PAINTING ∘ COLOR ∘ HISTORY

COLLECTION PLANNED AND DIRECTED BY
ALBERT SKIRA

GERMAN PAINTING

The Late Middle Ages (1350-1500)

TEXT BY HANSPETER LANDOLT
TRANSLATED BY HEINZ NORDEN

Only a few decades ago it was still possible to present a survey of German painting in the late Middle Ages in a single volume. Now that Alfred Stange's magnificent corpus of German painting in the Gothic Age is available in its entirety, eleven volumes, with more than 2,000 pages of text and 3,094 illustrations, an author—unless he be willing to content himself with a mere enumeration of artists' names and works—is left with the choice of either writing specialized studies of more limited subjects, or of treating the overall theme in the broadest outline, singling out only the high spots. For its contours have become much more diverse, much richer in detail. We must step farther away to see the countryside as a whole. From such a vantage-point some of the minor ranges and prominences that played their part in establishing the co-ordinates of the landscape when it was viewed close up tend to vanish.

To avoid misapprehension, the author should like to make it clear at the outset that he has accepted this limitation in full awareness of all that it means. Many names the reader is likely to encounter in the major museums he will find not even mentioned here. Indeed, he will look in vain for whole regional schools of painting that in the author's view are calculated neither to enrich the total picture nor to lend it greater diversity—for example, the short-lived colonial domain the Teutonic Order established in the Slavic East. The text, moreover, is to discuss, insofar as this is possible, only such works as the reader will find reproduced in this volume. A similar principle of self-imposed selection has indeed been employed with the illustrations themselves. The goal was not to give a little bit of everything but to present only what is crucial and significant, and that from as many aspects as possible.

Lastly, the author is bound to express his gratitude to many of his professional colleagues who have freely given counsel, suggestions, information and help of every kind; and above all to his beloved wife, Dr Elisabeth Landolt, who undertook the arduous task of sifting the literature and compiling the bibliography.

Hanspeter Landolt

Contents

Background
and Frame of Reference

Background
and Frame of Reference

WHEN we look out into the world, we tend to see it in bits and pieces that have no true objective character on their own. Just so, when we look back upon history, we are likely to grasp it only in segments that are in the main determined by our own intellectual outlook. It is meet, therefore, that any historical treatise, and more particularly one that proposes to deal with broad areas in space and time, should be preceded by a reasoned statement that sets forth why this particular area and era were chosen. The sole objective temporal unit in the total flow of history is the life-span of one man. As for objective spatial units, there really are none. The historian, in point of fact, does not deal with countries, regions and continents as such, but with "mobile" man who dwells in them and creates their history by his works. Yet it would be wrong to view the inescapable need for choosing a limited ground in the writing of history as nothing more than a necessary evil. There is no such thing as "history as such," only history seen through the eyes of man, interpreted by him. That is why history undergoes change far less by virtue of new facts unearthed in research than by new perspectives in approach and understanding. History changes as the generations give way, one to the next.

Three separate concepts enter into our theme, *German Painting in the Late Middle Ages;* and each of them on its own represents a segment of art history as a whole. Least ambiguous of the three is painting, which we shall discuss further within the context of the artist's special tasks. The term late Middle Ages is on a far less certain footing. Just when do these late Middle Ages begin, when do they end? It is true that the juncture between the Middle Ages and the Modern Age is marked by a whole series of incisive events and distinctions— a dividing line marked in our special case even more plainly by the starting point of the companion volume to this one, *German Painting from Dürer to Holbein;* but the onset of the period here singled out will vary widely, in keeping with the perspective that is chosen. In general terms of art history it is encompassed within what we call the Gothic style. In terms of painting it coincides with the great new challenge of the panel picture, which found its support in a new social class, the bourgeoisie. The time of this event in Germany was the mid-fourteenth century. Hence our era embraces roughly the century and a half from 1350 to 1500.

There is, lastly, the geographical term Germany, by far the most equivocal of the three. Indeed the whole business of subdividing Europe into massive regions, which has come to be the custom in art history, is at best dubious and subject to qualification. It is largely a backward projection in time of the emergence of national states that took place in the nineteenth century, when scholarship was first applied to art. None of these national states wholly coincides in area with the corresponding European countries in the late Middle Ages. In certain cases, such as the Netherlands, there is not even a semblance of such a thing—although there the lines may be justified all the better in terms of clear-cut regions, each with its own tradition in art. It is rather different in the case of France, although even her political frontiers in the late Middle Ages do not coincide with those of the nineteenth century, let alone the present day. In domestic and political terms, however, France was even at that early stage consistently tending in the direction of her later character as a modern national state. Italy, lastly, did not even exist in a political sense in the late Middle Ages, although there a common tongue did give rise to a "nation" in the intellectual and cultural sense, one that created an art entirely its own.

Not one of these prerequisites is to be found in late medieval Germany. Indeed we may well ask what that territorial term signified in the first place. Did it mean the Holy Roman Empire? That loose entity embraced sizable regions clearly owing allegiance to other cultures —almost all of the Low Countries, the Franche-Comté of Burgundy and, at least formally, a large part of Italy. Did it mean the area where German was spoken? That would have excluded major areas, Bohemia above all, where German culture was nevertheless a living presence. Or can a regionally contiguous complex with an art tradition of its own be identified, as in the case of the Netherlands? Here too the answer must be no, for the art of the Lower Rhine is more remote from the Tyrol than from the Netherlands, while Pacher has more in common with Mantegna than with the Master of St Bartholomew. Germany may be a familiar and quite unmistakable geographical concept to us today, but in late medieval terms it must be regarded as no better than a rather flimsy expedient, something of a makeshift. Yet we have no choice but to continue using the term, no better one being available. No harm in that, so long as we are aware of what Germany was like during the time in point.

Germany in the Fourteenth and Fifteenth Centuries

The bemusing diversity of German art in the late Middle Ages was closely reflected in the political situation. The extinction of the Hohenstaufen dynasty in the mid-thirteenth century marked the collapse of the supranational Holy Roman Empire, in thought and in fact; and with it went the inner fabric of Germany, so hard for us to grasp today. Thenceforth there was a consistent trend towards the emergence of a growing number of sovereign principalities within Germany. At the point in time where our scrutiny begins, about the middle of the fourteenth century, the crumbling of the Empire into petty sovereignties was actually codified in such international law as remained. With the Golden Bull of 1356, a kind of Imperial Constitution, Emperor Charles IV, at the cost of acknowledging the territorial sovereignty of seven Electors (including himself!), exacted the strengthened personal power he sought. Of no small importance in this development was the fact that the Pope, from whose hand the German King received the Imperial Crown of Rome, although in essence an outsider, retained legitimate scope for exerting his influence on the political sphere within Germany. This greatly favoured the arbitrary jurisdiction of the individual German princes.

In this connection a geographical fact that militated against German cohesion must be mentioned. In the East, at least, there was no natural frontier. Britain on her island had a coastline none could mistake. France's only open border, in the Northeast, was shared with Germany, with which France had once formed a single political unit under the Carolingians; but Germany lay wide open in the East, across the whole breadth of the continent. Not only were there no natural frontiers—there were no neighbouring countries that belonged to the European system of states as it had emerged from the Roman Empire. A marked cultural gradient, moreover, exerted its pull towards the Slavic East. Into the time of Charlemagne central Europe was settled and ruled by Slavs up to a line running from about Lübeck in the North to Trieste in the South, and the dominant trend throughout the Middle Ages at their peak was the steady German advance towards the East. Some Slavic regions like the Kingdom of Bohemia were taken into the Holy Roman Empire intact, others like Saxony and Silesia were conquered and Germanized, while along the Baltic Sea the Teutonic Order created a proper German colonial domain reaching to the Gulf of Bothnia, quite outside the Holy Roman Empire and with a curious political complexion of its own. At the same time the Hanseatic League established its trade dominion over the entire European Northeast. In the late Middle Ages this German eastward expansion not only ground to a temporary halt, but its outermost bastions had begun to crumble. German rule in the East was succeeded by Slav. The only Slavic country to remain with Germany was Bohemia.

The German princes who had exacted their sovereign rights in the Golden Bull were not the only ones to benefit from the dwindling power of the Holy Roman Empire. The cities did equally well. From the cultural point of view their growing power was indeed far more significant than that of the princes, who were able to make their courts once again centres of art and culture only at a later stage, in the Age of Absolutism. In the fourteenth and even more the fifteenth centuries, the towns and their burghers became the most important exponents of culture and, next to the Church, the major patrons of art. This development was by no means limited to Germany. We need only recall that the mendicant orders founded in the thirteenth century, such as the Franciscans and Dominicans, had relinquished the landed property that formed the economic base for the Benedictines in the earlier Middle Ages, settling instead in the cities and ministering in the main to the townsfolk. Indeed the flowering of the cities in Italy and the Netherlands preceded its counterpart in Germany. Yet in Germany this process followed a particular form that led to consequences of great significance to the history of art.

In the earlier Middle Ages the principal role of the cities had been to serve as fortified places where the peasants could seek refuge. Now they grew more and more into centres of commerce. The transition from barter to a money economy and the rising importance of trade and craft began to turn the cities into focal points of action. Political consequences were not slow to follow. By ransom or rebellion the townspeople asserted their independence from their territorial or episcopal overlords. But in Germany they were not quite the same people as in Italy and the Netherlands. In a general way we may say that in Italy and the Low Countries the dominant elements of the citizenry were the traders and that these lands shared a certain cosmopolitan outlook. In Germany, on the other hand, it was the craftsmen with their guilds who more and more set the tone. For them the city walls were above all else a barrier to competition from the outside. They guarded their economic interests by the institution of tightly organized guilds that exercised strict control over the practice of crafts. Art too was considered a craft, subject to guild jurisdiction; and in the towns it stood in far greater danger of becoming encapsulated and inbred than at the courts where artists summoned from far away constantly came and went. Eloquent testimony of this is afforded by the Prague court of Emperor Charles IV, who sent to North France, South Germany and Italy for his architects, sculptors and painters, and who maintained close relations with the papal court at Avignon. Another instance is Augsburg, the town of the famous Fugger family of merchants. After the middle of the fifteenth century it became the first outpost of the Netherlandish influence in German painting; and later on, soon after 1500, it was the gateway by which the Italian Renaissance invaded the North. Yet even in the smaller towns, especially numerous in South Germany, where the crafts predominated, art could not be altogether imprisoned within the spirit of intellectual pettiness. Masters from elsewhere could be admitted to guild membership, although it was more difficult for them to acquire citizenship. Then too the custom of journey-manship, under which craftsmen spent several years following their apprenticeship on the road, was the vehicle for much stimulating exchange in the arts.

The Artistic Challenge

At the height of the Middle Ages one can speak of painting as a separate art category only with certain reservations. Painting then meant murals, stained glass and book illumination, three genres that are quite different, even though they have much in common. Both mural painting and stained glass were closely dependent on architecture and their autonomy was therefore limited. Illumination was largely displaced by printing in the fifteenth century and thus scarcely qualifies as an elementary art form.

The late Middle Ages saw the development of panel painting, later to be modified into the framed painting on canvas that was to dominate the art of painting down to the early twentieth century. Actually the new type of the panel painting was not the outgrowth of a rising bourgeoisie that was flexing its muscles. It grew up under the aristocracy at the older courts. Yet it was the burghers who eagerly seized upon it and gave it currency as particularly appropriate for them. "Townsmen, being private individuals... have no churches nor castles built, commission no burial chapels or mural cycles. All that they order is altarpieces and panel paintings, and this they do in the hundreds and thousands" (Arnold Hauser). In the seventeenth century Dutch painting was to give convincing proof of the causal relation between the framed picture—the later form of the panel painting—and the bourgeoisie as the leading element in society.

Yet the reign of the panel painting over a span of five centuries proved to be far more enduring than the rule of the middle class, which was largely crowded off the political stage in the Age of the Counter-Reformation and Absolutism. There must have been reasons for this other than those rooted in the social order. Surely it is no accident that the dominance of the panel picture coincided in time with the dominance of naturalism in art—those five centuries during which art devoted itself to the representation of objective reality, showing even the supernatural in terms of natural perception. Stained glass subsisted on light, devoid of any semblance of the material world. Mural painting, like illumination, was largely an art in two dimensions, basically decorative rather than illusionist in character; but the painted panel was essentially an isolated visual record, a piece of reality into which one looked as through a window. Through all the changes in technique and the succession of styles over these five centuries, the panel painting remained true to the principle of representing visible and tangible reality. Art and reality had an inward and necessary connection. It is under this aspect that the late Middle Ages, the period that gave birth to panel painting, is of special interest.

Germany's share in this achievement is considerable, but it must be viewed against the broader background of the development of art in Europe as a whole. What accrues specifically to the credit of German and Netherlandish art, however, is the winged altarpiece that grew originally from the more or less modest shrines meant to hold holy relics. It developed into an ever more elaborate, free-standing, three-dimensional shrine that could be closed by means of hinged shutters—an example is Michael Pacher's high altar in the church of St Wolfgang. The extraordinary vitality of this species is probably explained from the fact that it was originally derived from several different forms, ultimately converging into a single type. The relative shares of wood-carving and painting in the development of the altarpiece, which remained highly variable to the very end, provide a clue in that direction. Only the exterior or verso sides of the wings were always reserved to the painter. Often, however, he would also do the insides of the movable wings, the fixed panels that flanked the shrine, the base or predella that separated the shrine from the altar proper, and even the central panel—although in other cases all or some of these elements might be given over to the wood-carver's chisel. There were many possible variants between the extremes of the altarpiece that was all carving and the one consisting solely of painted panels. The form most often chosen conceded the centre and the predella to the wood-carver and the wings to the painter.

The movable wings, often in two and occasionally even three pairs, lent these altarpieces a wealth of scope in form and orientation unequalled by any other type of altar art. This broad range made it possible to accommodate several picture cycles, each with numerous individual scenes, in a single altarpiece—e.g. the Passion of Christ and the Life of the Virgin. Yet the richness of these altarpieces with their changeable aspects is not limited to the multiplicity of figures and scenes that thus become possible but extends to the manner in which they could be differentiated. The opening and closing of the wings was prescribed by the liturgy. An altarpiece with several pairs of wings was fully opened only on high Church festivals; and on such occasions it was required to display its golden splendour in all its wealth, to render visible the highest elements of revelation. On ordinary days it remained closed, showing only its more modest workaday habiliments, often held down to grey-in-grey—what is called grisaille in art circles.

Polyptych altarpieces in Germany must have been vast in number at one time. There was an immense amount of church-building in the later Middle Ages, and a new church usually meant new altarpieces. Many old churches, moreover, were redone inside, and in all this work an important part was played by the gifts of the urban bourgeoisie that had but recently achieved affluence and prestige. Altarpieces, in particular those boasting wings, became not only the most important challenge to German art in the late Middle Ages, but the major art form in terms of sheer numbers. Most of the late Gothic carved figures and painted panels we are likely to come upon in our museums today were once part of some altarpiece, and they go far in giving us a representative picture of the fine arts of that period.

Outside the Church too German art in the late Middle Ages revolved largely about the religious sphere, even when it was plainly moving in the direction of the private—and thus secular—sphere. An important way-station along this road was the so-called devotional picture, meant to "afford the individual beholder occasion for contemplative immersion into the meaning of the religious theme depicted and to allow subject and object to blend into one, so to speak" (Erwin Panofsky). The origins of the devotional picture, which occupies a particularly important position in German art, must be sought in the mystical poetry of the late thirteenth and the fourteenth centuries. The subsequent shift of emphasis away from poetry and towards painting (and sculpture) is of great significance as an indication of the growing importance of painting generally in the late Middle Ages. Julius Böheim has traced a similar development in the changing response to nature and landscape. Devotional pictures were, of course, meant to serve for personal devotions; and to that end they often focussed on individual scenes or single figures from the great Gospel stories—Christ as the Man of Sorrows, the Virgin as a *Pietà*; or venerated traditional scenes such as the Madonna were invested with new feeling. In either case the earlier objectivity and austerity in representation gave way to a measure of human warmth hitherto unknown. Hand in hand with this humanization of the story of redemption went its wider dissemination in pictorial form. The art of printing, newly developed in the fifteenth century, became in its graphic forms the art of the common man, and it is not without significance that it paid special attention to the devotional picture.

The portrait provides perhaps the most impressive evidence of the degree to which the religious and the secular spheres overlapped and interacted in the late Middle Ages. Although the portrait, from the Renaissance onwards, was one of the secular challenges to art *par excellence*, it nevertheless grew up in the soil of religion, in which it remained rooted into the late fifteenth century. We do not here allude to the fact that donor portraits appear in altarpieces, or that subsidiary figures may be portraitlike in aspect. No, even outright portrait panels always expressly showed the sitter face to face with some devotional challenge—let the portrait diptych of Count Löwenstein with the Man of Sorrows serve as an example. It is true, however, as in this instance, that portrait and spiritual focus are usually quite distinct, without thereby becoming fragments in the aesthetic sense.

None of the other painting categories that were then new were able to develop such relative freedom and autonomy in the late Middle Ages—neither landscape, nor still life, nor genre. All were then only in the initial stages of emerging from the straitjacket of religious figure-painting into a life of their own. Soldiers were shown at their gaming and brawling at the foot of the cross; exquisite still lifes were inserted into the studies in which learned Church Fathers are seen; and light-drenched landscapes served as backgrounds for scenes from the lives of Christ and the saints.

The Regional Schools of Art

Except for the Slavic border regions in the East, particularly Bohemia, Germany was rather more uniform in an ethnic sense than, say, France with its population groups of varied Teutonic, Latin and Celtic extraction. Yet in a political sense France was ordained to move in the direction of a national state, while Germany tended towards particularism. Indeed the establishment and spread of ecclesiastical principalities at the peak of the Middle Ages marked a trend away from the original hereditary duchies, such as Franconia and Saxony. In art history, nevertheless, it is precisely these traditional and ethnically uniform geographic units that have gained a firm foothold as the basic regional schools. Such divisions are all well and good when they are used merely as relatively neutral geographical designations; but German art historians show a tendency towards ascribing to these regions certain inherent and unvarying characteristics, and this is, to say the least, dubious. It is true that there are such instances, but they form the exception rather than the rule. While some centres of art did manage to assimilate and reduce to their own common denominator all the influences that were brought to bear on them from abroad, others showed themselves quite incapable of forcing foreign trends into their own local mould. The order followed in this book is chronological rather than regional, but this will now be supplemented by a brief attempt to review German painting in the late Middle Ages by individual regions. The aim, however, is to bring out their contributions to the total picture rather than to characterize their artistic peculiarities, whatever they may be.

We shall begin our survey with *Cologne*, if for no other reason than that the late medieval painting of that town was the first early German "school" to come to modern attention, early in the nineteenth century. Cologne was the major centre of the Lower Rhine region, powerful in a political and economic as well as in a creative sense; and it forms an important exception in that its artistic fertility remained remarkably constant in the fourteenth and fifteenth centuries, while its art as such retained a clear-cut and constant local character. We are hard put to single out any periods within the late Middle Ages that could be described as times when painting in Cologne reached a particular peak, for it clung to a uniformly high level and showed an astonishing capacity for assimilating foreign influences and artists who came there from far away; yet the notably conservative character of Cologne painting severely limited its influence upon the total German development. Perhaps the time when that influence was most noticeable was during the period of the "Soft Style," when the Cologne style itself was most in tune with the dominant stylistic trend in Europe generally. Throughout the period covered in this book, as a matter of fact, Cologne itself was most strongly stimulated from the direction of the West and Southwest of Europe, and during the particular time here in point these regions were indeed the style-setters.

The seminal effect of Cologne art was most marked in the broad area between the Lower Rhine and the lower course of the Elbe, and beyond to Lübeck, although it was by no means continuously felt. There was no sharp line, in the sphere of art, between the two main regions of this area, *Westphalia* and *Lower Saxony*. Centres of Cologne's importance were lacking. Among the Westphalian towns Dortmund and later on Münster were probably the most productive, in terms of art. In Conrad von Soest, Westphalian painting reached a pinnacle it was never again to equal, although the breadth, concentration and continuity of its output are remarkable, as is the relative uniformity of its character. Precisely this last trait is absent in the painting of *Hamburg*, where two such utterly different artists as Master Bertram and Master Francke were able to unfold their talents in swift succession. In the second half of the fifteenth century this region clung particularly closely to Netherlandish art and for that reason accepted the Renaissance only at a later date, evidently from no sense of inward necessity.

We cannot speak of a school of art in the proper sense at all when it comes to the *Middle Rhine* region, which was more in the nature of a corridor, a link between Cologne and West-phalia on the one hand, and the Upper Rhine and Swabia on the other. No significant impulses seem to have issued from there. It is not without significance that the major Middle Rhenish artist of whom we have tangible knowledge, the Master of the House Book, had already attained firm creative stature when he came from far-off parts to the region of Mainz, where he did indeed meet with outstanding success.

The most powerful early German school of painting comprised the overlapping regions of the *Upper Rhine* and *Swabia* (which then included the now-Bavarian territories west of the river Lech). It numbered countless towns, large and small, most of them *reichsfrei*, i.e. owing allegiance only to the Emperor, and all of them filled with a fierce local pride—from Colmar and Basel in the West to Nördlingen, Ulm and Augsburg in the East. It was here that the urban bourgeoisie—among whom, in the fifteenth century at least, were to be found the most important patrons and cultural supporters of art—displayed the greatest concentration and power. Added to this came the two great Church assemblies, the Councils of Constance and Basel, which dragged on for many years, bringing money and artistic stimulation with them. All this helps us understand why the Upper Rhenish and Swabian school of painting began to flourish only in the bourgeois fifteenth century rather than as early as the fourteenth. In the first quarter of the fifteenth century the centre of gravity lay along the Upper Rhine, in Strasbourg and Basel, while in the second quarter it shifted to Swabia, and in the second half both regions were equally productive, together with Switzerland. From about 1420 onwards it was from Western Upper Germany that the commanding impetus emanated for the growth of art throughout Germany. Here too lay the mainspring of the graphic arts which—especially through the medium of the engraving—in turn reacted upon painting.

In *Franconia* Nuremberg played the same dominant role as did Cologne on the Lower Rhine. Down to the middle of the fifteenth century, the propinquity of Bohemia is very noticeable in Nuremberg painting, although the influence from that direction was absorbed and transformed with considerable independence. Yet Nuremberg was scarcely one of the focal points in the development. This changed only in the second half of the century, with the appearance of Pleydenwurff, who came from Bamberg and reminds us that that town was next in importance after Nuremberg as a Franconian art centre, and from whom a direct line leads to Dürer. With Dürer, the *praeceptor Germaniae*, Nuremberg, of course, became the artistic centre for the whole of Germany for a long time to come. *Thuringia*, bordering Fran-conia in the North, already belongs to the peripheral regions, in a creative as well as a geogra-phical sense. True, a whole series of paintings of great significance issued from the major Hanseatic town of Erfurt, which boasted a university after 1392, but as a rule these were works of artists who came from elsewhere. Thus no continuous tradition ever evolved nor did Erfurt become anything more than a local centre.

In *Bavaria* we encounter once again a region with a sharply marked character of its own. During the declining years of the fourteenth century Bavaria eagerly succumbed to the sweeping power of the art of neighbouring Bohemia, much as she did, in the second half of the fifteenth century, to Netherlandish naturalism, which was then flooding the whole of

Germany. Yet Bavaria managed to give these trends a coloration all her own. Drama, vehemence and expressiveness are the persistent elements in the art of Bavaria. Its peculiarity lies in the individual interpretation it gave to what it borrowed, rather than in the creation of new pictorial ideas. It can scarcely be described as one of the truly creative regions in the late medieval painting of Germany.

Present-day *Austria* fell into clearly distinguished divisions in the fourteenth and fifteenth centuries. One of them was the Duchy of *Styria*, a region closely connected with Bohemia, among other things by dynastic ties. An important element in its artistic development was the preponderance of ecclesiastical and dynastic strongholds and the absence of autonomous towns controlled by their citizenry. Hence we shall not be surprised to learn that the most important works from this region date from the time of "International Gothic," of the "Soft Style." A circumstance of some importance is that Hapsburg power reached all the way to the Upper Rhine, which favoured artistic exchange across great distances. Separated from Austria by the powerful sovereign bishopric of *Salzburg* lay the *Tyrol*, another region that had fallen under Hapsburg sway, but that abutted on Upper Italy rather than Bohemia. Indeed, in the last quarter of the fifteenth century the Tyrol became the very first entryway for the Italian style, primarily because of the great figure of Michael Pacher, who also worked for Salzburg patrons. This role lent Pacher fundamental significance in German art.

The mixed Slavic-German Kingdom of *Bohemia*, which included Silesia, harboured the only German school of art with its own history and unmistakable character. Hence there are valid reasons why the Czechs today should seek to exclude the art of Bohemia from the overall history of German art. Against the background of a unique political constellation and under a unique leader, Bohemia after 1350 moved towards an artistic flowering of incomparable power and grandeur. On the Slavic rim of the Empire a sun was rising that was to put all else in the shade, warming and fructifying the ground far around as well. Virtually every impetus underlying German painting about the year 1400 was of Bohemian origin. Bohemian painting, an art of clear-cut courtly character, around this time merged into "International Gothic" and what it brought to that style makes up an essential share of the Gothic substance. Inside the country, the Bohemian school kept on repeating itself until in the end, after 1500, it fell under the artistic sway of Nuremberg.

The Scholastic and Mystical Background

If there be any single basic element in German painting of the late Middle Ages, discernible in its every aspect, it is the struggle to master and represent reality. This reality might be the reality of sense experience—or it might be a spiritual reality; but whether of the outside world or of man's mind, it was always an art of the natural rather than the transcendental.

To comprehend the depth and ardour of the struggle for experiential realism in the late Middle Ages we must bear in mind the stake and the obstacles that had to be overcome to gain it. A passage from a source in late antiquity may serve to give us an idea. St Paulinus of Nola, who was born in Bordeaux in 353 A.D. and died in 431 as Bishop of Nola, was once asked for his likeness by a friend, the monk and historian Sulpicius Severus. "What manner of likeness shall we send thee?" he replied. "Is it to be of the earthly or the heavenly man? I know thou seekest the everlasting kind the ruler of Heaven loveth so deeply in thee." The central problem and challenge that confronted the art of the earlier Middle Ages are here expressed. This and this alone was the issue of iconoclasm in the eighth century, which was not at all aimed at an injunction against all images as such. Only that was worthy of representation to the early and high Middle Ages which was beyond representation, which could be expressed in symbols alone. This problem of incompatibility was very real for early Christendom, which encountered a rather similar art tradition of realistic representation when it arrived upon the scene. It found the solution, not in representational figure art, but in the conversion of that art into a kind of antirealism. The theological disputes over the question of Realism (then used in a different sense) versus Nominalism make it plain that this problem persisted into the high Middle Ages. Realism, the doctrine that ideas were the sole reality, held undisputed sway into the twelfth century—*credo, ut intelligam*, to know, I must believe. This transcendental system of thought and ideas was, of course, not merely mandatory upon theology but also served to determine the outlook of the individual. In the thirteenth century, however, the doctrine of Nominalism made inroads upon it, and in the fourteenth century it was at last toppled by William of Occam. To the Nominalists the so-called universals (ideas) were mere designations, names *(nomina)*, while the unique thing, rooted in individual sense experience, was accounted the only true reality. The victory of Nominalism meant the acknowledgment of the kind of reality that can be experienced and comprehended through the senses —and this victory was won by no means outside the Church nor in rebellion against it, but in its very bosom. It was owing to this circumstance that the theocentric absolutism of the high Middle Ages became transformed but slowly into the modern anthropocentric approach.

An important point, characteristic for the situation in Germany, is that this development, rather than being fostered by Rationalism, stemmed primarily from the religious movement of Mysticism. Its protagonists were the mendicant orders, hostile to Scholastic theology— the Dominicans and Franciscans—and the most important centres of the movement were the convents. The mystical predilection for Pantheist notions here too came to place a higher value on the instinctual, the natural, the individual. The new relation between man and God was significantly defined by the Dominican mystic, Master Eckhart (c. 1260-c. 1327): "God can do without us as little as we can do without Him." This may serve to explain why spiritual reality becomes so important in late medieval German art, which never seemed to go all the way in tackling the reality of the senses—that is to say, the individual object. One artist would be interested in facial features, another in the verisimilitude of the isolated figure, still another in figures arrayed in space; but the logical consummation of Rationalism—to comprehend a picture as such as a segment or metaphor of reality, to be subjected to the laws of nature—that final step was taken only by the Italians and the Dutch. This does not mean that the artists of these countries were more realistic than the Germans, only that they were realistic at a different level. It is under these special considerations that late medieval German art, and especially painting, are invested with such abundant diversity and dramatic tension.

The Royal Court of Bohemia
and Its Impact on Art

Master of Hohenfurth.
The Nativity, c. 1350. (37⅝×33⅝″) Panel from the Hohenfurth Altarpiece.
National Gallery, Prague.

The Royal Court of Bohemia and Its Impact on Art

IN growing from the flat decorative style of the high Middle Ages to the realism of the later stages, painting in Germany followed several roads. The crucial step, however, was taken in the time from 1350 to 1400 in a single place, Bohemia. What happened there was a phenomenon rare in Germany, for the art of Bohemia was closely identified with her Royal Court, indeed, developed in complete dependence upon it. It also shared the fate of that court in ultimately sinking back into humdrum provincialism.

John of Luxembourg, son of Emperor Henry VII, had acquired the Royal Crown of Bohemia in 1310, by marriage to a Bohemian princess. Their son, Charles IV, became Viceroy of Bohemia in 1333 and reigned from 1346 or 1348 until his death in 1378 as King of Bohemia, and Holy Roman Emperor. His personal domains extended far and wide, for in addition to his modest-sized Luxembourg patrimony in the West and Bohemia in the East, he also ruled over Moravia, Silesia, Lusatia and Brandenburg; and by descent and education he was a genuine cosmopolitan.

Charles IV made Prague for a time the intellectual and artistic centre of the whole Empire. In 1348 he founded the first German university in Prague, which became a meeting-place for scholars from all over Europe, and more particularly a unique point of contact between German and Latin West Europe and the Slavic East. To supervise the building of the Cathedral of St Vitus, begun in 1344, Charles summoned Matthew of Arras, a Frenchman from Avignon. Upon Matthew's death in 1352, direction of the project passed to Peter Parler, a German from Gmünd in Swabia. Charles's finest creation is Karlstein Castle, whose interior even today reveals the hand of an Italian artist, Tommaso da Modena; it is the most enduring memorial of a great ruler.

Charles's son and successor, Wenceslas, who ruled as Emperor until 1400 and as King of Bohemia until his death in 1419, was unable to preserve his country's prosperity. In the bloody and ruinous Hussite Wars Bohemia lost her place in the political and cultural forefront. Nor did the art of Bohemia survive these disasters. One element that may have been responsible, as has been true in other instances, was that royal patronage went largely to artists summoned to the Prague court from abroad. The effect of this influence served to inhibit rather than develop local talent, which remained quite unprepared to take on the full artistic challenge on its own.

The Hohenfurth Altarpiece

The Hussite Wars wrought havoc among the art treasures of Bohemia. The outstanding example of middle and late fourteenth-century painting in its earliest phase to survive consists of nine panels from the Cistercian collegiate church at Hohenfurth near Budweis (now Ceské Budějovice) in South Bohemia, a Gospel sequence done about 1350 and at one time probably comprising a large altarpiece. The panels, now separated, are an *Annunciation*, a *Nativity*, an *Adoration of the Magi*, an *Agony in the Garden*, a *Crucifixion*, a *Lamentation*, a *Resurrection*, an *Ascension*, and lastly a *Descent of the Holy Ghost*. They are variable in style and it is a moot point whether they represent the work of a single master who grew with his task, as is contended by Ernst and Stange, or whether they must be apportioned to several painters, as Oettinger maintains.

The panels that are most mature in terms of quality, the *Nativity* among them, display a sense of space that is wholly novel in the art of Germany. The background is composed of odd slabs of rock, and Worringer thinks this is derived from the "terrace landscape" of late antiquity. Here it rises towards a rather low horizon; yet it is not simply an unfolded stage flat, as is true of even the most advanced landscape backgrounds of earlier vintage; instead it is actually developed in three-dimensional depth. The stable is set slightly aslant, hence is also used as a three-dimensional element. The source of this new approach must undoubtedly be sought in Italy. Early in the fourteenth century Giotto had given new dimensions to the representation of space, by moving from a backdrop only sketchily suggested to a projection of continuous space. The Hohenfurth *Nativity* in particular shares some common traits with Giotto. Like Giotto's corresponding fresco scene in the Arena Chapel in Padua, it sticks to the Byzantine version of the theme, derived from the "cave birth," in which the mother is shown supine; and the airy stable bears a surprising resemblance to Giotto's in the Arena sequence.

From this "modern" realism, however, the Hohenfurth master retreats in his figure compositions, which are essentially in the decorative two-dimensional manner. For the most part the figures are arrayed in flat rows, sometimes of a stiffness approaching heraldic symmetry, such as in the case of the two figures preparing the bath in the foreground of the *Nativity*. All of the figures are really given life by the melody of their contours, the play of drapery, rather than by anything that could be called a tangible, physical presence. This aesthetic approach too the Master of the Hohenfurth Altarpiece may have absorbed from the art of Italy. His inspiration is unlikely to have been the astringent realism of Florence, but rather the more delicate air of Siena, which stood in the odour of having "better taste"—or perhaps the outposts of Sienese art at the Papal exile in Avignon.

This special aesthetic response also dominates the treatment of the inanimate. Now and then subsidiary elements in the pictures combine into still lifes of haunting beauty. They have nothing whatever to do with the religious symbolism of the high Middle Ages, which saw man only as created in the image of God, and to which all material things stood only as tokens of an invisible world. They are equally remote from the robust, sensory realism that marked the bourgeois painting of the fifteenth century. What is presented here is the kind of reality that offers itself to the cultivated aristocrat, savouring art like a good wine.

Some further works have come down to us from this earliest phase of Bohemian painting during the reign of the Luxembourg dynasty, notably the *Glatz Madonna* in Berlin, the most important early Bohemian painting in any collection outside Czechoslovakia. This large Madonna panel was evidently the centre of an altarpiece which the Archbishop of Prague, Ernest of Pardubice, gave to the Augustinian monastery he founded in 1350 in the North Bohemian town of Glatz (Kladzko). This Prince of the Church, one of the great figures in the

Master of Hohenfurth.

The Agony in the Garden, c. 1350. (37⅜×33⅝″) Panel from the Hohenfurth Altarpiece. National Gallery, Prague.

reign of Charles IV, is shown in the lower left-hand corner. When Charles separated Bohemia from the Archbishopric of Mainz in 1344, creating the Archbishopric of Prague, Ernest of Pardubice became its first incumbent. He died in 1364 and lies buried in Glatz, where he grew up and owned estates. The altarpiece he commissioned was probably done in the 1350's, presumably in Prague, as was true of the earlier Hohenfurth altarpiece. The panel is of large size (73¼ by 37⅜ inches) and shows Virgin and Child against an excessively elaborate structure.

It is the Throne of Heaven, flanked by angels and the lions of the Throne of Solomon. Yet the austere symbolism is violated in certain particulars. Two small angels have pushed open the shutters and are swinging censers out the windows, a detail that is anything but austere but rather conveys the friendly aspect of a doll's house. In formal terms this throne is a delicate architectural conceit, a piece of decorative veneer rather than a solid piece of architecture. The central group of Virgin and Child still bears the outward marks of the Byzantine tradition, but has cast off its aloof severity in favour of a new sense of naturalness. One has only to regard the language of the hands, or the figure of the donor, who has quite nonchalantly

Bohemian Master.
Virgin and Child Enthroned (Glatz Madonna), c. 1350-1360. (73¼×37⅜″)
Gemäldegalerie, Staatliche Museen, Berlin-Dahlem

Bohemian Master. Diptych with Christ as the Man of Sorrows and the Virgin and Child, c. 1360. (12×7½″ and 12×7⅝″)
Öffentliche Kunstsammlung, Basel.

doffed the insignia of his office and set them down before him, before himself kneeling down. In the matter of such small, homely touches the *Glatz Madonna* goes beyond the formalism of the Hohenfurth panels.

The *Glatz Madonna* is testimony and expression of the kind of mariolatry to which Ernest of Pardubice and even his king, Charles IV, were dedicated with a fervour occasionally heightened to the visionary stage. This Virgin worship left its mark on contemporary religious literature in Bohemia as well. It was not, however, the exclusive prerogative of the aristocracy and the educated, but wide-spread among the people as well. This explains the curious circumstance that in Bohemia the image of the Virgin came to take on a life of its own in art. A few Madonna types created in the fourteenth century remained almost immutable, like icons, and were repeated over and over again, down into the eighteenth century. In Bohemia too the Madonna became a devotional picture—an example is a diptych, done about 1360 and now in Basel, that shows the Virgin, in a not very common iconographical type, in combination with a Christ as the Man of Sorrows. The devotional character of this panel is unmistakable. The Virgin with the Child caressing her is meant to appeal to the sentiment of the devout rather than to their faith, and so, quite clearly, is the image of the suffering Christ beside her. Both love and suffering are symbolized with marvellous effectiveness by light and shadow. Another element adds to the significance of this diptych. It retains its original frame, which includes a small reliquary. This too recalls Charles IV, who is known to have been an almost fanatical worshipper of relics.

Theodoric of Prague

The finest monument to Charles's relic worship is Karlstein Castle near Prague, which serves as a setting for the most important works of the second phase of Bohemian painting. Romantic in aspect, the castle was begun in 1348 by Matthew of Arras, architect of the Cathedral of St Vitus in Prague, and it became the repository for the treasures of the Holy Roman Empire as well as the Emperor's own reliquary. Its core is the Chapel of the Cross, consecrated in 1367 and located within the castle keep, which dominates not only the castle as such but the whole countryside. Numberless semiprecious stones of substantial size are set into its gilt walls, which are surmounted by a star-spangled vault glittering with gold. With its haunting magic, the chapel almost physically conjures up the presence of the ruler for whom it was built, in all his sombre grandeur.

The outstanding decorative element of the Chapel of the Cross are 129 large panels recessed into the walls, showing the Crucifixion, Christ as the Man of Sorrows and half-length figures of saints, angels and prophets. The identity of the master responsible for them is known. He was Theodoric of Prague, painter to the Imperial Court and member of the Prague painters' guild. What remains uncertain is whether he was a local man or an artist summoned from abroad. The distinguishing mark of his style is the emphatic corporality of his figures, although he seems less concerned with their three-dimensional articulation than with their sturdy, ponderous, massive and rather shapeless bodies as such. Like the Master of Hohenfurth, he too attacks sensory reality; but he substitutes the physical mass of the body for the sheer exploration of space. In his quest for ways of lending expression to the impact of reality, he too seems to have gone to Italian sources, particularly in the person of Tommaso da Modena, who was born about 1325 and worked chiefly in Modena and Treviso, and who contributed three works to the decoration of Karlstein. Whether he actually came to Prague to do them or whether the panels came from abroad is a question that has not been settled to this day. His style is less diffuse and inarticulate than Theodoric's, but he too dwells strongly on the experience of physical presence.

The most important individual work in the distinctive style of Theodoric is the *Votive Picture of Archbishop Jan Očko of Vlašim* in the Prague National Gallery. It is a tall rectangular panel, the upper half of which shows the Virgin enthroned between St Sigismund and Charles IV on the left and the Royal Prince Wenceslas with his patron saint on the right. The lower half of the picture shows the archiepiscopal donor kneeling in the middle, flanked by Sts Procopius, Adalbert, Vitus and Ludmila. A remarkable feature is that the royal personages, while shown on their knees, are of the same relative stature as the sacred figures. As in the busts in the triforium of the Cathedral of St Vitus in Prague, done at about the same time, this betokens the rising secular self-assertion that marked the early stages of Humanism; and it also lends expression to the increasingly sharp challenge of realism. Hence there is a certain consistency in the fact that, in formal terms, tangible bodies have become more important than abstract linear patterns. One need only compare the figure of the Virgin with the *Glatz Madonna*. The nervous, delicately-limbed lady has become a plain and unassuming handmaiden. There is an inkling that her body really has weight beneath the heavy fall of its drapery, even though its articulation is not revealed. Another logical development is that the donor's head bears the aspect of a portrait. Jan Očko of Vlašim, by the way, was elevated to the archbishop's throne of Prague in 1364, succeeding Ernest of Pardubice, of whom we have already heard; and we thus know the earliest date at which this votive picture can have been done.

We can scarcely be surprised that the next step, leading to the practice of portraiture for its own sake, was also taken at this time and in the circle about Theodoric of Prague. The earliest specimen in the whole of German painting that has come down to us is a small

Viennese Master (?).

Portrait of Duke Rudolf IV of Hapsburg, c. 1365. (19×12¼″) Diocesan Museum, Vienna.

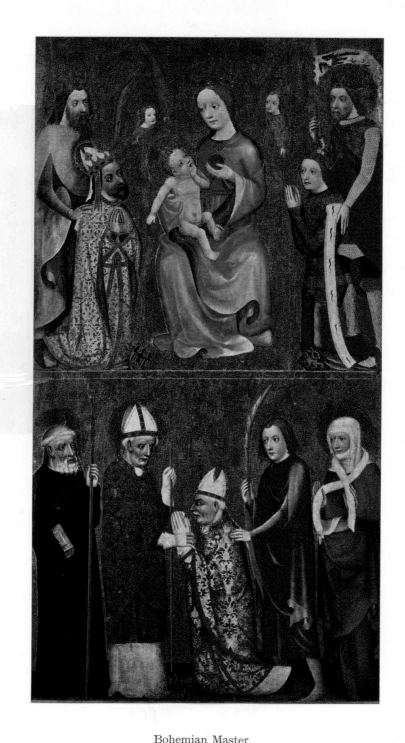

Bohemian Master.
Votive Picture of Archbishop Jan Očko of Vlašim, shortly after 1364. (71¼×37¾″) National Gallery, Prague.

panel in the Diocesan Museum at Vienna with the head of *Duke Rudolf IV of Hapsburg*, the talented and rebellious son-in-law of Emperor Charles IV. This panel is today believed to be the work of a Viennese painter who entertained relations with Theodoric of Prague, a connection rendered all the more plausible by the sitter's close blood ties with the Prague Court. As founder of the University of Vienna, the Duke, who died in 1365, was known as Rudolf the Founder. In the portrait, his face shows the same blurred and doughy softness as the heads in the Karlstein panels and the Vlašim votive picture. Yet the reason why the features lack sharpness must be sought, not in any predilection of the painter for the typical and impersonal—which has on occasion been imputed to him—but rather in his own peculiar approach to comprehending the sitter's character. It is not a "lesser" individual statement, merely a "different" one. Buchner has aptly compared this portrait with the approximately contemporary one of King John the Good in the Louvre, the earliest known French portrait painting, which shows the sitter in sharply accentuated—indeed, almost exaggerated—profile. The contrast between the two pictures underlines the sombre character of the German portrait incunabulum.

Master Bertram (c. 1340-1414/15). The Creation of the Animals. Wing Panel of the Altarpiece of St Peter's, Hamburg (Grabow Altarpiece), installed in 1383. (33⅞×21⅝″) Kunsthalle, Hamburg.

Master Bertram (c. 1340-1414/15).

The Agony in the Garden, after 1383. Scene from the Central Panel of the Altarpiece of the Passion. (20½×20″)

Niedersächsische Landesgalerie, Hanover.

Master Bertram

In the same way as the Imperial Court at Prague became the cynosure for royalty throughout Europe in the second half of the fourteenth century, so the Bohemian school was the model for painters elsewhere in Europe, at least within the domains of the Holy Roman Empire, where it exerted a stimulating and creative effect. Almost everywhere, and especially in the immediately surrounding areas, regional schools of painting began to take on the Bohemian cast. This influence, moreover, impressed itself on the style of the only contemporary painter of transcendent stature and unmistakable character outside of Bohemia,

Master Bertram of Minden, who flourished in Hamburg. Here we have perhaps the most convincing evidence that the role of leadership assigned to the Bohemian school is indeed legitimate. It attained this role not in solitary grandeur, but wrought its spell in another soil as well, far to the West.

The name of Master Bertram is not a mere empty tag. He is one of the first truly tangible figures in the history of German art. Born probably about 1340, he came from Minden in Westphalia to Hamburg, where he died in 1414 or 1415. After 1367 his name recurs again and again in documents, most prominently as the master of the high altar installed in Hamburg's Church of St Peter in 1383. This double-winged altarpiece was rediscovered only late in the last century in the town church of Grabow in Mecklenburg—and for that reason is sometimes described as the Grabow Altarpiece—whence it entered the Kunsthalle in Hamburg. It is Master Bertram's *chef-d'œuvre*, and beyond that the most important work of art of the North German Trecento. It is preserved in almost its entirety—only the paintings on the exterior sides of the outer wings are lost. Both wood-carvers and painters took part in creating it. Fully opened, it is over 23 feet wide, and its assemblage of 79 carved figures place it among the richest of all works of sculpture. With the inner wings closed and the outer pair open, it displays a cycle of 24 painted panels. Sculptures and paintings are closely akin in terms of style; but since the sources expressly describe Bertram as a painter, we have no particular reason to regard him as the carver as well, even though the late Middle Ages did know instances—such as that of Michael Pacher—when the two talents were combined in one man

The panels of the Altarpiece of St Peter's deal with the Creation, the lives of Adam and Eve and their sons, the story of Isaac, and lastly the early chapters of the Gospel story, from the Annunciation to the Flight into Egypt. The peculiar style of Master Bertram is shown in its purest form in the Creation panels. On no less than seven occasions the Almighty here dominates the picture, his figure filling the panel almost to its full height. Always carefully set off from the environment, the monumental figure of God looms up into the gilt ground, "huge and solitary, like a letter in braille," to cite Worringer. Even in the other scenes, where figures are combined into groups, these do not enter into any real contact with one another, but tend to rest in themselves. Vigorous of body, robust of hand, large of foot, they project the reality of the human form in a manner altogether new in German art, at least outside Bohemia. In this respect Bertram's realism is closely related to that of Theodoric of Prague, although Bertram voices the common primary intention in another idiom. His figures are active and articulated, even supple, rather than massively shapeless and passive like Theodoric's. What that means in formal terms is that in their overall appearance and their postures, in their contours and the fall of their drapery, Master Bertram's figures are pervaded by a sense of tension and rhythm.

West and East here impinge upon each other, in terms of their different ways of life and creative principles, to be blended into a new alloy, through the personality of a great artist. Scholars have differed in their assessment of the share the Bohemian element contributed to this blend—indeed, any such share has often been disputed outright. Yet there was no other possible model for Bertram's dramatic three-dimensionality than the Bohemian style of Theodoric. It is precisely in this point that Bertram has nothing in common with the several Westphalian precursors that have been cited time and again—the altarpieces in Netze and from Osnabrück, now in Cologne (two works that cannot even be proved to have preceded the Altarpiece of St Peter's in time), and the altarpiece in Schotten. It must be remembered, moreover, that in those days Hamburg was virtually neighbour to the Luxembourg realm, hence in a manner of speaking to its heartland of Bohemia as well. The Brandenburg line lay no more than sixty miles upstream from Hamburg, along the Elbe River. And contact with the cities of the Hanseatic League was the main goal of Charles IV's economic policy.

Master of Wittingau.

The Resurrection, c. 1380-1385. (52×36¼″) Panel from the Wittingau Altarpiece. National Gallery, Prague.

The Altarpiece of St Peter's is the most important and voluminous among the works of Master Bertram that have come down to us, but it is not the only one. Many others unmistakably bear his stamp, although their authenticity is disputed. This is true in respect of the altarpieces from Buxtehude and Harvestehude, both now in the Hamburg Kunsthalle; the panels in the Musée des Arts Décoratifs, Paris, which have gained new interest in the light of certain newly discovered miniatures in Bertram's own hand; and the Altarpiece of the Apocalypse in the Victoria and Albert Museum, London. All these are plainly cruder works, outclassed by far by the panels of an *Altarpiece of the Passion*, undoubtedly by Bertram's own hand, that went from private ownership in England into the Niedersächsische Landesgalerie in Hanover in 1929. This piece was almost certainly done after the Altarpiece of St Peter's. In it a greater preoccupation with the narrative has softened the painter's obsession with the isolated human body—and this cannot be explained solely from the fact that the events depicted are themselves more dramatic. In any event, the result is that the pictorial elements are more successfully integrated. The sketchy indications of locale in the St Peter's piece—rather in the manner of the Shakespearian stage—are now spatially elaborated. An illuminating device is the fence that entirely surrounds the group composed of Jesus and three Disciples, in the *Agony in the Garden*, hemming them in closely and thus adding a spatial effect to the plastic quality imparted to the figures. This synthesis of the Hohenfurth and Theodoric styles is of great significance to the subsequent development of German art. It was certainly not achieved within the Bohemian school itself—indeed, perhaps, could no longer have been achieved there, because that school lacked the requisite Western sense for the dialectical relation between body and space. The student here parted ways with the preceptor who had inspired him and struck out on his own—and this is a process that applied beyond the individual case of Master Bertram. Yet Bohemia's great mission in the history of late medieval painting was not yet fulfilled. During the final phase of its time of grandeur, the Bohemian school was to push open one more door, to make one more dimension accessible to the art of Europe.

The Master of Wittingau

The achievement just hinted at already falls into the reign, beginning in 1378, of Charles IV's hapless and mediocre son Wenceslas. It emerges chiefly in a number of panels, some of them belonging together while others show a close stylistic relationship, that have reached the Prague museum from the South Bohemian town of Wittingau (Třebon). This provenance has resulted in their putative author being called the "Master of Wittingau."

The two most important panels may have been the wings of an altarpiece in the Church of St Giles, which was attached to the Augustinian monastery in Wittingau. The church was not finished before 1380 and the panels were presumably done in the early 1380's. On one side they show an *Agony in the Garden* and a *Resurrection*, on the other *Sts Catherine, Magdalen and Margaret* and the *Apostles James the Less, Bartholomew and Philip*. There is no way of telling what the altarpiece as a whole looked like.

The Passion scenes are placed in a setting of spatial depth. In the *Resurrection* this space is evoked, in the first place, by the oblique position of the coffin, and this diagonal is taken up and countered in the landscape background by the opposing diagonal of the ground formation. Yet the space is not a constructed artifice—it is real enough, something actually seen and reconstituted through the medium of painting. The shadowy depths hold some richly animated landscape details, but these are not actually developed from the foreground, and their precise location in space cannot be verified. Still, their living reality in space is much more strongly projected than, say, the rationally drawn landscapes in the Hohenfurth Altarpiece. The irrational element of colour here serves as a creative means to a degree without

Master of Wittingau.

Sts Catherine, Magdalen and Margaret, c. 1380-1385. (52×36¼″) Panel from the Wittingau Altarpiece.

National Gallery, Prague.

precedent; but the message itself also avails itself of colour. The miracle of Christ's Resurrection in the flesh is rendered plausible, not by physical realism as such—it is proclaimed by the beacon of his red cloak, glowing against the dark.

Even the sense of movement is here not so much realistic as it is expressive in character and meaning; and this is the crucial operative term for this final phase in the Bohemian school of painting of the Trecento. The Hohenfurth phase may have conquered the element of spatial dimension, the Theodoric phase that of physical mass; but to the Master of Wittingau must go the credit for having first staked out in the art of painting the full expressive scope of form. It is true that in his disembodied figures—a peculiarity that leaps to the eye when his work is compared with the style of Theodoric—and in his cultivation of a sense of line he already approaches the "international" or "soft" style that was to dominate all European art in the

Bavarian Master.
Christ on the Cross between the Virgin and St John, c. 1390. (70×53¾″) From the Augustinian Church, Munich.
Bayerisches Nationalmuseum, Munich.

first quarter of the fifteenth century; yet in contradistinction to that style, the linear element in the Master of Wittingau is eminently expressive in its meaning rather than denoting a purely aesthetic preciosity. All the expressive trends in the time to come go back to him. Indeed one may fancy one finds a late echo of his heritage even in Grünewald.

It is significant that this Bohemian expressionism had a very swift and enduring effect in neighbouring Bavaria. As will be shown, a great need for expressiveness seems always to have formed part and parcel of Bavarian art, which was fond of resorting to dramatic and vehement means. Preserved in the Bayerisches Nationalmuseum in Munich is a panel, done about 1390, from the Augustinian Church in that city, a *Christ on the Cross with the Virgin and St John*, which unmistakably goes back to Bohemian models and ideas. Here too a "serpentine line" underlies the composition as a whole, but it is a line of painful writhing rather than of pictorial music, an expression of the mind that is at once suggestive in itself. In a surprisingly modern sense, this suggestive form is used not merely where it is immediately appropriate, to wit in the figures. No, it projects the emotional tone of the characters, so to speak, reaching out into the neutral environment—the winding path, for example. Rather than organizing the space between the figure group and the horizon, this serves the function of enhancing the mood by echoing the formal theme of the figures. It is from the Master of Wittingau too that the painter of the Munich panel has taken over his characteristic manner of painterly structure, working his way from dark towards light.

We shall have repeated occasion, in the pages that follow, to point out how the Bohemian school served as a model to German painting in times to come; but the works in point will always date back to the fourteenth century. In the fifteenth century the focus of growth shifted to the West, and ultimately, in the Age of the Reformation, the Bohemian school, insofar as it had not simply become stagnant, continued to speak merely in a Southeast German or Franconian dialect. The curtain had fallen on Bohemia's role of greatness in the history of European art—at least until the intermezzo of Rudolfinian Mannerism, when once again, for a brief space, Prague was to become the great intellectual and creative fulcrum of Europe.

The "Soft Style"

The "Soft Style"

FOR the time being the shift in the focus of the development of art from Bohemia to the West did not at all mean that the Bohemian school, which had been dominant in Germany for something like five decades, was succeeded by another, delineated with equal clarity. What happened instead was that Bohemian painting merged into a larger all-European stream. We are confronted with a very curious, indeed almost unique phenomenon in the history of Occidental art. For a while—not longer than a quarter-century—artists spoke a common tongue, whatever its various nuances may have been. Its essential characteristics were aristocratic refinement, an uncorporeal translucency, unworldliness and a marked preference for the musical flow of form. We hear it in the painting of Siena and in that of French Burgundy. It was spoken in Westphalia and Cologne, just as it was in Hamburg and Prague. In recognition of this agreement, the term "International Gothic" or "International Style" has been applied to the art of Europe for the approximate time-span from 1390 to 1420. It forms the larger framework for what has been called, in terms of German art, especially sculpture, the "Soft Style."

Viewed in the light of the daring achievements of a Giotto or a Theodoric of Prague, International Gothic was a decidedly reactionary phenomenon. Its delicate and ethereal women were recreations of figures from the age of the minnesingers, long gone. Looking at its fine-limbed men in their precious armour, one would never imagine that their real-life counterparts were bleeding to death on the battlefields of Europe, fighting the infantry of modern mass armies. The artist's hand, which had already reached out for reality, was for the nonce withdrawn. Once again the glow of fable and an almost wistful lyricism held sway. Measured against the historical facts of the time, this style is almost quixotic in character. Perhaps that term sounds too harsh, but it does serve to render International Gothic more comprehensible. Like Cervantes's Knight of the Rueful Countenance, it was remote from reality, indeed at odds with it, while in a loftier sense transcending reality. The crucial element International Gothic shares with Don Quixote is that it created a new and utterly real life of its own beyond ordinary reality, against which it rebelled without illusions. In similar circumstances and as the outgrowth of a similar crisis, the nineteenth century was to give rise to what the Germans have come to call *Kitsch*, tasteless and pretentious productions that project wishful images devoid of real life. International Gothic, by contrast, was still a valid and living art form. Only those who insist that growth must always be in a forward direction will regard it as a fleeting and regrettable regression.

International Gothic demonstrates its basic soundness not least by its immunity to the danger of drying up or becoming frozen. Down to its finest ramifications, and even in border-line cases like the work of Master Francke, it remains full of throbbing life; and in this respect it is quite different from the Gothic Mannerism of the late fifteenth century. Nor did it come to an abrupt end, moving instead organically into the art of the great realists of the 1430's —in the Netherlands the Van Eycks.

The Soft Style was an art of the aristocracy which, obeying some inner necessity that called for a stylized way of life, was bound to create an appropriately stylized art. Within such parameters of culture and mind—described so inimitably by Johan Huizinga in *The Waning of the Middle Ages*—art could not but follow this road, take this "step back-wards." If it, nevertheless, avoided the danger of lapsing into sterile archaism, if indeed the very cult of the abstract carried the seeds of the realism that was to supervene in the second quarter of the century, this surely goes to the credit of the major role the bourgeoisie played in the whole development. The courts were, of course, the great centres of art—Paris, Dijon, Prague—but besides them there were also great cities, where art flourished on a foundation of industry and commerce, and where the patrician class struck the cultural keynote—places like Florence, Cologne, Hamburg and the Flemish towns.

International Gothic, then, came to life all over Europe, a kind of lingua franca spoken by artists of every land and clime; but this did not rule out the formation of clear-cut focal points. The most important were the courts at Paris and Dijon, the latter exerting a powerful influence on those regions of the Low Countries under Burgundian sway. The result, in German terms, was that the provinces impinging upon France and the Netherlands came to the fore —the Lower Rhine and Westphalia, with fringes reaching all the way to Hamburg and a bit later the Upper Rhine as well. Another vital artery led from Prague into Southeast Germany, notably Vienna, and by the time the Soft Style had about ended its reign also to Nuremberg. The middle zone of Upper Germany—chiefly Swabia—flanked by the two regions of greatest significance in terms of the Soft Style, was at this time only storing up the great creative energies that were to come into full flower in the second quarter of the century.

The Southeast and Nuremberg

Of the German regions fringing Bohemia, it was the Southeast, all the way to Nuremberg —actually no farther from Prague than Vienna!—that articulated the International Style most plainly and with an unmistakable Bohemian accent. Since the Trecento painting of Bohemia had many facets, its impact and emulation could lead to very diverse results. We took note of this in our discussion of the fourteenth century. The art of Master Bertram and the *Christ on the Cross* from the Augustinian Church in Munich are both unthinkable but for the example of Bohemia, however different they may be. The store of paintings that have come down to us is meagre, and we can actually discern with any degree of clarity but one focal point or school, in Vienna, or rather Wiener Neustadt, the whilom residence of the Dukes of Austria. There are also a larger number of isolated works that are very hard to place into an even approximate geographical context; for during the decades of International Gothic the overall characteristics were much more marked than those peculiar to any one particular region. In only rare instances, such as the *Imhoff Altarpiece* in Nuremberg, do we know even the identity of the donor, which gives us at least the location for which the work was intended.

The most important early fifteenth-century Southeast German work gives us an idea of these difficulties—the *Pähl Altarpiece* in the Bayerisches Nationalmuseum in Munich. Salzburg, Munich and Augsburg have all been mentioned as possible places where this mar-vellous piece was done, yet there is no convincing link with any of these art centres, in the

South German Master. Christ on the Cross between the Virgin and St John, early 15th century. (40¾×26¾")
Central Panel of the Pähl Altarpiece. Bayerisches Nationalmuseum, Munich.

Austrian Master (?). The Throne of Mercy (or The Trinity), 1410-1440. (46×45½″) Central Panel of an Altarpiece.
By Courtesy of the Trustees, National Gallery, London.

form of other paintings known beyond doubt to have originated there. What speaks against Munich is its radical departure from the other work, typically Bavarian in its expressive vehemence, with which we are already familiar—the *Christ on the Cross* from the Augustinian Church in Munich. The Augsburg theory is based on the fact that Pähl, near Diessen on the Ammersee—where the altarpiece is supposed to have stood in the Castle Chapel and where it was acquired in 1857—belonged to the Bishopric of Augsburg. Nor is it even established that the altarpiece was intended for Pähl in the first place. The most plausible hypothesis, proposed by Alfred Stange and according with the overall artistic context of the time, holds that the *Pähl Altarpiece* is the work of a migratory artist who moved from Prague to the West.

44

It is of rather modest size, no more than four feet high. The central panel shows *Christ on the Cross*, flanked by the Virgin and St John the Evangelist, the left wing *St John the Baptist* and the right one *St Barbara*. On the verso of the wings, in a poor state of preservation, are a *Christ as the Man of Sorrows* and a *Virgin and Child*. The artistic point of departure is quite evidently the style of the Master of Wittingau. The Crucifixion scene follows him not merely in general terms but quite literally; and all ebullience is studiously avoided, as in the Wittingau panels. The differences derive in the first place from the lapse of time of something like two decades, and then from the distance between the places of origin. In the later and westernmost work the forms have become more arbitrary and decorative, and by the same token less expressive. The figures are on display, so to speak—St John the Baptist, for example— exhibiting a kind of noble serenity, shallower and less mysterious than their Bohemian kin. Like the Master of Wittingau, the painter of the *Pähl Altarpiece* has a rich painterly instrumentarium at his disposal, differentiating his palette in finely graduated nuances. Overall it is lighter, less sombre, in the literal as well as the applied sense. If the Master of Wittingau gives us a polished dialogue, what we have here is a kind of silent monologue.

The rather large and self-contained group of works seemingly painted in Vienna and Wiener Neustadt come considerably later, hence are more strongly permeated with International Gothic—which means, conversely, a greater departure from the Bohemian models. On one of them, a *Christ Carrying the Cross* in private hands in Linz, an obscure signature, "Johan," can be made out; and in consequence Karl Oettinger has associated the whole lot with Hans von Tübingen, evidently a painter of considerable note, who is mentioned on numerous occasions in Wiener Neustadt from 1433 until his death in 1462. The paintings do indeed bear a highly individual stamp, and one is tempted to accept the attribution to a master who, from the available sources, played a major role in the painters' guild and at the Ducal Court, and whom one would like to see as the head of a school; but the last word has not yet been said on this matter. The fact that Hans von Tübingen was still living in 1462 persuades us to date the whole group rather later than the stylistic findings would really indicate. On the other hand, one of these works, the *Epitaph to Siegmund Waloch, Goldsmith of Wiener Neustadt* in Hennersdorf Castle, can scarcely have been painted earlier than 1434, from an inscription and the identity of the persons represented; and we come to see that in this peripheral region the International Style survived for a surprisingly long time—indeed, into the time of the great realists Multscher and Witz. Thus there is considerable uncertainty as to the proper chronological order of this important group of Austrian paintings in the Soft Style.

This is true also of the splendid and radiant masterpiece in the National Gallery, London, the *Throne of Mercy*, in our view an early work. Older scholars have regarded it as coming from France or the Rhineland, and various dates ranging from 1410 to 1440 have been assigned to it. Almost square in format, it was originally the central panel of an altarpiece, the two wings of which may be the panels with saints, preserved in Rastenberg Castle. The pictorial structure of the central panel is lucid and austere, almost mathematical in character. The Almighty is seen in straight frontal view, seated at dead centre on an elaborately constructed throne and holding before him the Crucified Christ, towards whom a dove is descending. On either side is a praying angel.

Every detail in this realization of the Trinity is exquisite—the colour chord of gilt ground, white, unearthly shimmering throne, and complementary red-green of robes and angels' wings; the melodious flow of line, especially the rising pyramid of the Almighty's mantle. On no other occasion did the art of Southeast Germany come so near to the formalism and cultivated taste of International Gothic. We are reminded of the small two-part early fifteenth-century altarpiece that was in the Heiligenkreuz convent in Lower Austria until it was acquired by the Kunsthistorisches Museum in Vienna in 1926, and that is unmistakably French in origin. Such works, imported from the West—if indeed they were not done by French artists

Austrian Master.
Votive Panel of St Lambert, 1420-1440. (37¼×72″) Landesmuseum Joanneum, Graz.

who actually came to Austria—may have caused the pendulum to swing towards the typical forms of International Gothic. Whenever this influence slackened or was absent, the affinity with the Bohemian style at once came to the fore again.

It becomes particularly manifest in the famous *Votive Panel of St Lambert* in the Landesmuseum Joanneum in Graz, probably done in the 1420's or 1430's and ascribed by Oettinger to Hans von Tübingen. On the left the Virgin with her protective cloak is shown beside a holy nun, on the right the battle of King Louis the Great of Hungary against the Turks. There is not a trace of courtly elegance here. The robes of the two female figures on the left are quite unmelodious—the drapery folds are thick and heavy, almost brittle. The teeming battle scene on the right nevertheless accords well with the tranquil, posed group with the Virgin, for it is altogether lacking in illusionist traits, rather being cast in an abstract, carpet-like plane. The arrangement is tasteless, pervaded by a sense of diffuse movement, a concatenation of swirling combat scenes. This alone would not betray the propinquity of Bohemia; but the kinship with the style of Theodoric does shine through in the massive aspect of individual figures and groups and in the aversion to delicate articulation. Perhaps, if more works in the Theodoric style had come down to us, we might have been able to find Bohemian parallels even to the languid vehemence of the St Lambert votive panel. Even so there is an echo of Bohemia in its curious minor key, quite foreign to the West, and in its unfathomable gloom.

We come upon the Bohemian mood, approach and idiom once more, in Nuremberg. We should bear in mind that the great free city in Franconia had close ties with Charles IV. His son and successor was born there in 1361, and he also endowed the Church of Our Lady on the market square. We are told that works of art from Bohemia reached Nuremberg as late as the first quarter of the fifteenth century; and certainly the two major works of the Nuremberg school during this period can be properly understood only against a Bohemian background. They are a wing of the *Deichsler Altarpiece*, done before 1419 and now in Berlin, and even more importantly, the *Imhoff Altarpiece* in the Church of St Lawrence, which was donated between 1418 and 1422. Both works reflect several currents in fourteenth-century

Bohemian painting, and in consequence they are almost eclectic in character. The heavy, massive, isolated figures of the *Imhoff Altarpiece* with their unnaturally short limbs follow the Theodoric style of the 1360's, while the calm and spiritualized features have their closest kin in the panels of the Master of Wittingau. Yet the forbidding aloofness of Bohemia has here become the gravity of the solid citizen. There is one surprising feature. One might have expected that at this historic juncture, around 1420, just before Multscher appeared on the scene, the ponderous three-dimensional solidity of the Theodoric style would have served as a springboard for an even higher degree of three-dimensional realism; but this did not happen—it was simply echoed in quite anachronistic fashion. The overwhelming impact of the Bohemian example is certainly evident here. The Nuremberg school was simply not yet ready to face the creative problems of the day.

Nuremberg Master.

Christ Crowning the Virgin. (46½×30¼″) Central Panel of the Imhoff Altarpiece, donated between 1418 and 1422.
Church of St Lawrence, Nuremberg.

Conrad von Soest (traceable 1394-1422).

Calvary, 1403-1404. (62×62″) Main Scene of the Wildungen Altarpiece.

Town Church, Bad Wildungen (Waldeck), near Cassel.

Conrad von Soest

That the emergence of Master Bertram as a reasonably discrete artistic personality in North Germany about the turn of the fifteenth century is not an exception, owed to chance tradition, is shown by Conrad von Soest, whose life-span actually overlaps Bertram's. We have a whole group of more or less authenticated works from the brush of Conrad, two of them indeed signed and one dated; and he appears frequently in the archives of the town where he flourished, Dortmund, one of the most powerful Westphalian cities in the Hanseatic League; for Conrad's geographical cognomen seems to be a family name rather than designating his place of origin. In any event, there is a record of his marriage in Dortmund in 1394, and he is repeatedly mentioned there between the years of 1413 and 1422. In 1420, moreover, he created his most mature work to survive for the Church of St Mary in Dortmund. The fame of his exemplary work spread by the trade routes that led from that town to Hamburg and the Hanseatic centres in the Northeast as well as to Cologne in the West.

Conrad's most impressive work, preserved intact at the place for which it was originally intended, is an altarpiece in the town church of Bad Wildungen in the Principality of Waldeck. When the single pair of wings are opened, the total width is no less than 24 ½ feet. The heart of the central panel is a *Calvary*; this scene is flanked on either side by twelve representations from the life and afterlife of Christ—extending from the *Annunciation* to the *Last Judgment*—arranged in two rows, one above the other. On the verso of the wings appears a memorable inscription that perpetuated the names of the painter and of the incumbent pastor, as well as the date of origin—1403 or 1404, the final numeral having become indistinct. The very fact of this then unusual information is a manifestation of the spirit of the new century, just begun.

Conrad's *Calvary* is peopled with a large cast of characters, demonstrating that he was thoroughly familiar with the scope of spatial composition that had been newly opened up. The figures are grouped in depth, overlapping one another to a considerable extent, and the possibilities of a three-dimensional stage have been notably utilized. The painter was mindful of the new realism—in the way he hid the root of the cross behind a slight rise in the ground that creates a sense of depth, in the crosses of the two Thieves, shown in oblique perspective. A number of mannerisms, however, blunt the impact of these devices and rob them of their full meaning. The clearest clue to the artistic intention is perhaps provided by these two Thieves' crosses, which succumb to a decorative scheme, despite their perspective. They rise near the centre of the stage, but Conrad allowed them to project above and beyond the limits of the realistic scene, utterly defeating its sense of realism. The observer notes that the oblique position of the crosses was not really intended to support the illusion of depth, but merely to round off the composition in the literal sense. Indeed, throughout the picture the abstract melody of line is stronger than the objective statement. The soft flow of the figures —especially those arrayed in brocade—joins with the plant life, the main lines of the terrain and the banderoles to form a rich and splendid tapestry.

The shapes of the individual figures are also fitted into this general scheme. Some years ago Rolf Fritz, using the infra-red camera, was able to reveal the painter's outline drawings hidden beneath the pigment layer. They show us a *bel canto* of unexcelled purity. In the soft flow of their self-indulgent lines, they seem almost oblivious of their object, the human body; and even spiritual reality, not merely the physical, is sublimated into a pallid semblance of itself. The sorrowing gestures of the three women beneath the cross seem to be dictated by etiquette rather than grief. Robert Nissen's findings support this impression. On closer scrutiny the seemingly expressive pictorial motives —the hands, for example—turn out to be based on a very limited spectrum of recurring patterns. They are not nearly as individualized as one might think.

Conrad von Soest (traceable 1394-1422). The Nativity, 1403-1404. (28¾×22″) Scene from the Central Panel
of the Wildungen Altarpiece. Town Church, Bad Wildungen (Waldeck), near Cassel.

Yet there is a deep gulf between Conrad's anti-realism—and indeed the anti-realism of International Gothic as a whole—and that of the high Middle Ages, especially in its Latin variety. The latter employed realistic motives solely as symbols that pointed to the transcendental, whereas Conrad, about 1400, sublimated reality. Far from negating it, he idealized and transfigured it. His art is not, properly speaking, religious—it toys with beauty for its own sake. Indeed, he adds a specifically German element to this secular general denominator—that intimate element Worringer has described as "genre realism pervaded with lyricism." One of its paradigms is the *Nativity* scene in the *Wildungen Altarpiece*. There the stable pre-empts the whole picture area, in contrast to the corresponding scene in the *Hohenfurth Altarpiece*, where it stands free in the countryside. Conrad draws the beholder inside, gives him a sense of homely shelter. The scene takes on the character of a family event, not least by virtue of the touching zeal with which Joseph is pursuing his domestic chores. The style of the Franco-Flemish courts is thus recast in terms of the private commoner; and this is indeed the German nuance of International Gothic—here we see the beginnings of that parlour intimacy so characteristic of German painting in the later fifteenth century. In the wake of aestheticism as such, a second step has been taken away from the Middle Ages and in the direction of the Modern Age; and of the two steps it was certainly the more unequivocal and decisive—the one that was to have the larger consequences.

The early works of Conrad von Soest show a closer kinship with International Gothic than the later ones. Ingeniously arranged robed figures like the fine *St Paul* in the Alte Pinakothek, Munich—the convincing attribution of which to the master's oeuvre we owe to Alfred Stange—or the controversial *St Nicholas* panel in Soest and the triptych with *Sts Dorothy and Odilia* in the Landesmuseum at Münster in the end give way to graver figures, more

Conrad von Soest (traceable 1394-1422).
St Paul, early 15th century. (20¾×7½")
Alte Pinakothek, Munich.

ponderous and monumental in character, but the most important piece in which we encounter Conrad's late style is the *Altarpiece of the Virgin* in Dortmund. Its three parts, a central panel and two wings, were cruelly mutilated during the Baroque Age, but much of their grandeur survives, even in fragmentary form.

The road Conrad von Soest traversed from the *Wildungen Altarpiece* and the small *St Paul* panel, both done early in the century, to the Dortmund *Altarpiece of the Virgin*, some twenty years later, follows the overall evolution of art. In Conrad's youth the influence of Europe's great art centres was the dominant element; and no doubt the close relations he entertained with the leading merchants in Dortmund were of great help to him in establishing contact with the art and artists of France and Burgundy, and perhaps even Italy; for his own creative growth is all but inconceivable without such contact, to which he probably owed his familiarity with the aristocratic, international art idiom of Europe. It was from that he developed his own individual accent which, as it happened, struck a key reminiscent more of Master Bertram than of his unidentified preceptors in Paris and Dijon. This is consistent with the impression that Conrad's art fed on many faraway sources, while it in turn did not wield nearly so wide an influence; but that limitation does not mean that it was lacking in impact and fire. What happened was that Europe was becoming compartmentalized—a trend that, among other things, ultimately led to the formation of national states. In art too the international lingua franca was being replaced with national tongues.

Cologne

In tradition, splendour and grandeur Cologne was the leading city of medieval Germany; and it was here that the Soft Style found its most receptive and fertile soil. The art of Cologne had always been essentially conservative, hence it eagerly seized hold of the conservative essence of International Gothic. In another aspect, however, Cologne painting during the period in point never reached the degree of overblown refinement encountered elsewhere, perhaps because it drew support from an element far broader than a royal court. In the early years of the fifteenth century Cologne grew so completely absorbed in projecting her own life in her art that in the course of the next hundred years or so she began to lose contact with the mainstream. The art of Cologne took on a coloration all its own.

One of the most noteworthy characteristics of late medieval painting in Cologne is its anonymity. Countless masters must have plied their art in this wealthy and art-loving town, yet not one of them saw fit to put his name to his work, not even the one whose name, at least, has been handed down by tradition, Stefan Lochner, who happened to be a "foreigner" from Swabia, at that. We should scarcely be surprised at this, for it concretely reflects the whole anonymous character of Cologne painting in the fourteenth and fifteenth centuries. The grip of convention was stronger in Cologne than elsewhere, the criterion of collective taste more important. There was a total absence of that search for the individual approach which the times seemed to demand, that compulsive urge to come to grips with new creative problems. The story-telling picture, on which much zeal was lavished in the more progressive regions, was not among the preferred categories in Cologne. There are rare exceptions, like certain scenes in the *St Clare Altarpiece* in Cologne Cathedral, done about 1400 and sharing some of the features of genre realism we noted in the *Wildungen Altarpiece;* but the two dominant categories were the devotional picture and the solemn ceremonial scene. They represent the dominant temperamental traits in Cologne painting: serene tranquillity and contemplative self-absorption—the "over-ripe sweetness of the Gothic outlook," as Glaser put it; and on the other hand a detached but not altogether aloof sense of solemn occasion. In a century when art as a whole was ardently devoted to apperception, the art of Cologne remained dedicated to the inner life.

By its highly individual character, rather out of step with the times, and indeed almost hostile to the present, Cologne art delimited itself more and more sharply from other German schools. Early in the century it still maintained close ties with neighbouring regions, notably Westphalia and Lower Saxony; but the isolation soon grew. It is a task fraught with extraordinary difficulty to distinguish within the total body of Cologne art clear-cut groupings, let alone to assign the rather large corpus of surviving works to major masters and their workshops. Art scholars have made many vain attempts in that direction, beginning with the lyrical legend of Master William of the Romanticists.

The concord in idiom, to be sure, does not bespeak a uniform level of artistic quality. A number of major works stand head and shoulders above the rest, to a degree that has made them virtually the epitome of Cologne art. We may perhaps assign pride of place to *St Veronica with the Sudarium*, an early fifteenth-century panel from the Church of St Severin in Cologne, now in the Alte Pinakothek in Munich. The Saviour's sombre countenance on the pallid cloth is scarcely marked with pain, but neither is it frozen into the rigidity of an icon. It is bracketed, moreover, betwixt jubilant and gently transfigured beauty — up above the girlish features of the saint, set against a partially ornamented gilt ground; and down below in the corners rejoicing child angels. All inward expression is foregone. Veronica, elegantly holding the kerchief, seems to be utterly detached from the token of martyrdom she is displaying. She gazes ahead, lost in thought. The two groups of three angels each might have been borrowed from some genre scene. Their playfulness seems quite unmotivated. Composition and colour scheme are of extreme sophistication. The daintiness of the saint's pose is further enhanced by the all but imperceptible departure from rigid symmetry, especially the varying level of the hands, which lends a slight irregularity to the drooping kerchief (in contradistinction to the somewhat drier copy in the National Gallery at London). A sense of counterpoint invests the two groups of angels. Oblique rear views alternate with oblique frontal views; and this rhythmical alternation also dominates the distribution of light and dark within the picture. The saint's pale face is framed in a deep red cloak that comes over her head, while the darkling features of the Saviour are set against the light ochre of the cloth. The beholder is spared the importunity of torment. The picture rewards the devout without challenging his faith. Nor is there any inkling of physical realism. Wilhelm Worringer once remarked ironically that one could scarcely bear looking at the picture, once one had asked oneself what St Veronica's figure and posture behind the sudarium could be like. Yet this is not a question to obtrude itself, for within its own frame of reference beyond all illusion of reality the picture has complete validity.

Numerous other works of the Cologne school, dating from the first third of the fifteenth century, have been ascribed to the Master of St Veronica, including one of the best-loved among all the creations of late medieval German art, the so-called *Madonna of the Sweet Pea* in the Wallraf-Richartz Museum in Cologne, in which the Virgin is shown flanked by Sts Catherine and Barbara. We shall not here risk entering the thickets of attribution, which are all but impenetrable especially in the domain of Cologne art and have yielded more thistles than figs. It should not be glossed over, however, that even Conrad von Soest has been suggested as the author of the *Madonna of the Sweet Pea*. Indeed, there is a theory that it should be regarded as a Cologne copy after a small portable altarpiece by Conrad von Soest, one wing of which has survived in the form of the small *St Paul* panel in Munich. In sum, the intent is to find a bridge that would link the art of Cologne with that of Westphalia.

The *Madonna of the Sweet Pea*, often bracketed with her virtual twin sister in the Germanisches Nationalmuseum in Nuremberg, is a devotional picture of purest water. With wings closed, this small altarpiece shows a *Christ Crowned with Thorns*. When it is open, the Virgin, Child in arms, appears between the two female saints like a fleeting dream image. All physical realism has fled from the figures. The crossed arms scarcely seem to touch, any more than the

Master of St Veronica (active in Cologne around 1400).

St Veronica with the Sudarium, early 15th century. (30¾×18⅞″) Alte Pinakothek, Munich.

Child's caressing hand seems to touch his mother's chin. One expects the features to express individuality, but instead they all dissolve in a kind of sweet emotionalism. The elaborately posed hands of the two companion figures become no more than accompanying arabesques, like coloratura passages. The art of Cologne could scarcely go farther in that direction.

When one envisages the historical background against which such intimacy of feeling condensed into pictures, one perceives discrepancies that seem all but irreconcilable. The whole latter third of the fourteenth century in Cologne was marked by the bloody dispute between the noble families and the rising middle-class, which ultimately carried the day. We may well ask which of the two social classes boasted these blissfully delicate and lyrical poems in paint. Did the artists stem from the *arriviste* artisan class or from the emasculated nobility?

Any attempt to assign a proper place within the art history of Germany and Europe to the early fifteenth-century art of Cologne must necessarily take account of its westward orientation. Its cultivated taste, lyrical character and steadfast rejection of realism inexorably tie it to the West, which in the case means not merely Paris, Dijon and the Burgundian Low Countries but even England; for English book illumination had not been without influence

Master Francke (traceable 1400-1425). The Miracle of the Wall, early 15th century. (37⅜×21¼″)
Wing Scene of the St Barbara Altarpiece. National Museum of Finland, Helsinki.

(Overall view of the altarpiece on page 150)

in Cologne. This Western substance was further differentiated under the influence of forces from the North, especially from the direction of Westphalia and Conrad von Soest. At the same time Cologne was one of the few German regions to remain utterly untouched by the long-range effect of Bohemian art. Wilhelm Worringer has tellingly remarked that Cologne art not only escaped the sense of tension between East and West characteristic of Central European art about 1400, but rather appears in the guise of a connecting link, or rather a seam between North and South.

Master Francke

In the late medieval art of Cologne collective characteristics were predominant, while the personal and individual share was comparatively slight. In the art of Hamburg the precise opposite prevailed. It displayed virtually no consistent and dominant local traits that might have given rise to a tradition, while it boasted two masters of towering stature, with a marked individuality found scarcely anywhere else at the time. We have already made the acquaintance of the first of these masters, Bertram. In the fifteenth century he was followed by Master Francke. Both were citizens of Hamburg by adoption. In terms of their life spans, it is at least conceivable that they may have both lived there at the same time for a while. It is all the more surprising that there is not the faintest trace of the earlier master's great achievement in the work of the later. The focal points of artistic development in Europe had shifted in the meantime. The crucial element in shaping Bertram had been the Bohemian art of the Theodoric generation. Francke, on his part, was profoundly influenced by the courtly art of France and Burgundy, and by its German variant, epitomized especially by Conrad von Soest. Francke's eyes were fixed on the West. At one time he was believed to be identical with a certain Henselin of Strasbourg, mentioned in Hamburg documents after 1383; and although this hypothesis has now been shown to be untenable, it does hold a solid core of truth, at least in respect of the general direction of Francke's artistic origins.

Actually, we do not know when nor whence Francke came to Hamburg. His name appears for the first time in 1424, as the recipient of a commission for an altarpiece given by the Company of Traders with England. Major portions of this altarpiece have come down to us. Using these as a point of departure, it has been possible to ascribe to him with assurance a work done considerably earlier, the *Altarpiece of St Barbara* in Helsinki. Francke's oeuvre has also been enlarged by the addition of two representations of *Christ as the Man of Sorrows*, one in the Kunsthalle at Hamburg, the other in the Leipzig museum. Two altarpieces and two individual panels of comparable merit—surely this can be but the leavings from a life's work that must have been originally very much larger. Yet this slim oeuvre bears the marks of a vigorous individuality, reveals to us a character unlike almost anyone who came before. It is for that reason that Master Francke has been spared the proliferation of ascriptions, more or less warranted, that forms such a popular and grateful game among art historians, especially in the field of early German painting. Francke's works stand before us in marvellous and unequivocal definition.

The *Altarpiece of St Barbara* came to the National Museum in Helsinki from Nykyrko in Southwest Finland. Beyond that point it cannot be traced with certainty. It is an altarpiece with a dual transformation, i.e. it has two pairs of wings. Fully open, it shows scenes from the life of the Virgin, in wood-carving. When the inner wings are closed, the outer ones being left open, eight scenes from the martyrdom of St Barbara—after whom the altarpiece is named—come into view. Two of these have always aroused amazement and admiration, a *Miracle of the Wall* and a *Betrayal of the Shepherd*. In both the painter allows a magnificent landscape to take possession of the picture, renderings that clearly show their descent from French miniature painting. The gilt ground is reduced to a narrow strip at the upper margin.

Master Francke (traceable 1400-1425).

The Scourging of Christ. (39×35″) Wing Scene of the Altarpiece of the Traders with England (or St Thomas Altarpiece), begun in 1424. Kunsthalle, Hamburg.

Master Francke (traceable 1400-1425).

The Murder of St Thomas à Becket. (39×35″) Wing Scene of the Altarpiece of the Traders with England

(or St Thomas Altarpiece), begun in 1424. Kunsthalle, Hamburg.

Master Francke (traceable 1400-1425). The Murder of St Thomas à Becket (detail). Wing Scene of the Altarpiece of the Traders with England (or St Thomas Altarpiece), begun in 1424. Kunsthalle, Hamburg.

If these landscapes nevertheless fail to create the illusion of space, this is largely owing to the figures, in the arbitrary treatment of which the artist has blithely ignored the laws of perspective. In the *Betrayal of the Shepherd*, the pursuers of the fleeing saint in the middleground are given several times the size of the shepherds in the foreground; and in the *Miracle of the Wall*, the pursuers loom above the ramparts of a tower of several storeys. One is tempted to view these violations of verisimilitude as typically medieval draughtsmanship, or as suiting size to inner significance; but such an interpretation overlooks that the painter was quite familiar with perspective in an empirical sense. The turret in the *Miracle of the Wall* is drawn with lines that converge in almost perfect perspective; and the landscape against which the Shepherd's betrayal is enacted recedes with equal realism. The artist would rather seem to have staged all these "blunders" quite deliberately, in order to dramatize his story and enhance the feeling of tension within the picture, the latter consideration undoubtedly being given precedence. The formalism of International Gothic is here, in the hands of an impulsive painter, suddenly turned in a new direction, beyond the prevailing conventions. The manner in which the wall, in the miracle picture, both in terms of its role and its shape, is made the dominant element is thoroughly characteristic of the Mannerist style. It is only from this aspect that the *Altarpiece of St Barbara* can be properly understood and assessed. It is Mannerism, not in the sense of "manneredness," of playful, detached, proliferating form, but Mannerism as demon-ridden form.

It is of the essence of Mannerism that it is incapable of being developed further, that it represents the final phase in an evolutionary sequence. This is borne out even within the oeuvre of Master Francke, as shown in his second major work, the *Altarpiece of St Thomas*, sometimes known as the *Altarpiece of the Traders with England*, probably begun late in 1424 and now in the Hamburg Kunsthalle. Like its predecessor in Helsinki, it boasts two pairs of wings, but in contradistinction every part of it is painted. Preserved are the inner wings and part of the large central panel, but an eighteenth-century engraving does at least give an idea of the themes of the lost outer wings. Full-open, the altarpiece showed five scenes from the Passion. With the inner wings closed, an upper tier gave four scenes from the life of the Virgin, while underneath four further scenes detailed the life of St Thomas à Becket, patron saint of the Hamburg Company of Traders with England.

Compared with the *Altarpiece of St Barbara*, the St Thomas work is more earnest, rugged and monumental in character. It foregoes the bold tricks and emphasis of the earlier work. It makes a more archaic impression. Bella Martens, to whom we owe the most comprehensive and searching study of Master Francke, has been tempted to conjecture that in the St Thomas work too the artist harked back to French models, but to older ones than he used in the St Barbara piece. Actually, we have no need of such a theory to understand why the dominant lines of perspectives are here drawn less vigorously, the landscapes given less feeling of space, the figures arrayed less conspicuously—flying in the face of the general trend and hence of historical logic. Young Master Francke was not out to conquer the world of reality. He was seeking to explore his scope in terms of form. Foregoing the elements that have been enumerated meant no step backward, even though it did not point towards the future. That it was nevertheless "progress" of a kind is shown by the fact that the later panels have a more haunting quality. None who has ever seen the *Adoration* is likely to forget its majestically enthroned Virgin; nor, in the *Scourging of Christ*, the dialogue between the doubt-torn Pilate and the suffering Saviour, played out to the full gamut of expression; nor the power of some of the faces, even though they are quite lacking in drama and pathos, e.g. the monks in the *Murder of St Thomas à Becket*.

Thus we see Master Francke growing towards greater simplicity and inwardness, in close accord with the development of Conrad von Soest. We are led to believe that this is not a purely personal parallelism, but rather the paradigm for the German variant of International Gothic.

Middle Rhenish Master.

The Adoration of the Magi (detail), c. 1420. Right Wing of the Ortenberg Altarpiece. Hessisches Landesmuseum, Darmstadt.

(Wing reproduced in its entirety on page 150)

Alsatian Master. The Crucifixion (detail), early 15th century.
Presumably from the Church of St Martin, Colmar. Musée d'Unterlinden, Colmar.

(Panel reproduced in its entirety on page 150)

The Middle and Upper Rhine

We have already come to see the regional schools and centres of Northwest Germany —Westphalia, Cologne—as forming a focal point of the Soft Style in painting. It remains for us to turn our attention upriver along the Rhine.

The *Ortenberg Altarpiece* in the Hessisches Landesmuseum at Darmstadt, probably done in Mainz around 1420, is the most important example of Middle Rhenish painting. It is a triptych of medium size, on the main panel of which appears a rare combination of two themes, the Virgin visited by her female relations, and the Virgin among virgins, i.e. surrounded by holy women. When the altarpiece is open, the central panel is flanked by an *Adoration of the Child* on the left wing and an *Adoration of the Magi* on the right. We can perceive that the unidentified master of this altarpiece was in direct or indirect touch with the courtly centres of International Gothic, from the richness and modish elegance of the dress, the carefully arranged and ostentatious hair styles and the mannered cultivation of posture and gesture. Further evidence lies in the employment of numerous motives that entered the French pictorial idiom from Italy via Avignon. Like the exponents of courtly panel painting, the Master of the Ortenberg Altarpiece foregoes all spatial and three-dimensional illusionism and aspires to flat, decorative tapestry effects. Also along this line lies the technical peculiarity that makes this altarpiece quite unique, the generous use over wide areas of gold and especially silver foil as a ground. Oddly enough, the effect is not one of barbaric splendour. The translucent, enamel-like paint almost seems to lose its material quality against the metallic background, and the pictures seem flooded in shimmering light. International Gothic is here given one of its most interesting and singular forms. As far as we can judge, however, it is a highly individual form, not one characteristic of the region.

Along the Upper Rhine we encounter a school of painting that is quite unmistakable and peculiar only to this region. It is true, however, that here too, as with the London *Throne of Mercy* for Southeast German painting, there is a major predecessor work that belongs to the International Style rather than any particular region: the early fifteenth-century *Crucifixion* in the Unterlinden Museum at Colmar. This richly peopled picture follows a well-established compositional scheme. Yet certain figures in it, surprisingly, have a form all their own, for example the officer beneath the Thief's cross on the right, who turns his back on the viewer, or St John with his sweeping and somewhat over-dramatic gesture. It is hard to avoid the general impression that a pointed and stylized scene is being enacted here, as on a stage, a feature reminiscent of court etiquette. The outward demeanour of the figures also points in this direction. They are shown either in highly mannered Burgundian court dress—the hem of the man at the right margin is even set with foppish, tinkling little bells—or in drapery cascading down in marvellous order. There are French parallels to many of these motives.

The *Crucifixion* at Colmar seems to come from the hoary town church of St Martin, hence always to have had its home in the Upper Rhine region. Yet it is difficult to establish a connection between this work and other local productions, and Otto Benesch has assigned it to the Austrian school, pointing out that the Imperial Town of Colmar was surrounded on all sides by outlying Austrian possessions—the Sundgau and the Breisgau. He rightly observed that the *Crucifixion* seems "in a peculiar way a work detached from all the schools, one in which Western, Northern and Eastern trends are blended." Unlike the great majority of German paintings in the Soft Style, it stands revealed as a work of International Gothic.

Soon afterwards the regional character of Upper Rhenish art asserted itself, in a group of paintings the most important of which are the *Joyous Garden (Paradiesgärtlein)*, the *Madonna of the Strawberries* at Solothurn, an *Annunciation* at Winterthur and the two panels from St Mark's at Strasbourg. Their common characteristics are the absence of courtly

glamour, a straightforward and almost secular sense of intimacy and a lyrical mood combined with a naïve and wholesome joy in the visible world. Each of these traits either forms a link with some other German region or draws a line against it. Taken together, they make up the unmistakable character of Upper Rhenish painting about 1420. The undisputed *chef-d'œuvre* of this group of paintings is the *Paradiesgärtlein* in the Staedelsches Kunstinstitut at Frankfurt, probably done in a Basel or Strasbourg studio. The Virgin in an enclosed garden *(hortus conclusus)* was a familiar theme of convent mysticism. Here the garden is given an added paradisiac dimension, in which spiritual and secular elements are curiously blended. The narrative itself is of the spirit. All the figures, and even the trees, plants, animals and objects, are integrated into a symbolic frame of reference of redemption; but the locale itself, the stage, so to speak, is rather in the nature of a formal garden, a courtly plaisance, than of an unearthly Elysium. It is a Decameron scene translated into Swabian terms. In posture, gesture and feature, the figures are neither individualized nor particularly expressive. Their round heads and small eyes, their noses and mouths stamp them all as members of the same family. We meet its members in several other panels, large and small—the small format was especially popular in this region at this time. Kurt Bauch was the first one to note that we find them even in popular woodcuts. These heads are indeed the leitmotif of Upper Rhenish painting in the Soft Style.

Upper Rhenish Master.
The Annunciation, c. 1420. (7¼×6″) Oskar Reinhart Collection, Winterthur.

This special vision of paradise in the *Paradiesgärtlein* in Frankfurt, together with the demeanour of the two well-groomed male figures on the right, certainly betrays a familiarity with courtly manners; but apparently this element was quite fortuitous, and it is not seen at all in so conventional a religious scene as the small *Annunciation* in the Oskar Reinhart Collection at Winterthur.

With its marvellous red-blue colour harmony, this precious little panel—it measures only 7¼ by 6 inches—stages the event in a rather cramped and sparsely furnished parlour. The perspective is very nearly perfect, and the picture frame is used like a window, allowing the viewer to peer into a realistic interior. Yet this treatment of space somehow does not seem like a radical departure from the medieval tapestry style. The effect is one of almost genre-like intimacy, derived from the carefully detailed background that is used to enhance the mood of the scene. The whole picture is pervaded by a sense of childlike grace and serenity, as in the work of the contemporary Fra Angelico. Like his Italian counterpart, the Upper Rhenish painter seems to shrink from the complete acceptance of realism, which indeed impended and is heralded here. He cannot bring himself to take it for granted. There are still insistent and persistent overtones of unworldliness. This little *Annunciation*, by the way, also enters into the world of prints. There is an engraved copy by the so-called Master of the Nuremberg Passion.

The two panels that have reached the Musée de l'Œuvre Notre-Dame in Strasbourg from the local Hospital of St Mark are distinguished from the works just discussed precisely by their greater willingness to come to grips with the formal challenge of the time, which in evolutionary terms means realism. One of them shows the *Education of the Virgin*, the other *Joseph's Doubts*. The chilly, monumental architecture in the former creates an instant Italianate impression, and this is confirmed by certain motives that are clearly borrowed. We must indeed conclude that despite the seemingly regional character of Upper Rhenish painting, it maintained contact with the art of Italy about 1420. The panel of Joseph's doubts (i.e. doubts of Mary's virginity) constrains us to compare it with the *Annunciation* at Winterthur. In both pictures the bourgeois interior shows many similarities. Yet in the Strasbourg panel it is

Strasbourg Master.

Joseph's Doubts, c. 1420. (45×45″) From the Hospital of St Mark, Strasbourg. Musée de l'Œuvre Notre-Dame, Strasbourg.

presented in much more aggressive and emphatic fashion, despite many "errors" in veri-similitude. A slender pillar of square cross-section blocks the view into the room. Tables, benches, chests, boxes, books, tools are all placed athwart and at sixes and sevens, in a calculated attack upon flatness. This gives the room an air of noise and bustle quite unsuitable to the graceful, tranquil and lyrical figure of the Virgin, who is shown entirely as the old familiar type. In the *Annunciation* the accent lies on the figures and the sense of intimacy that issues from them, while here the picture's character is determined by the harsh struggle for a new realism. To conquer reality in this way and bend it to the purposes of painting was to be the great task facing the next generation in Southwest Germany.

The Great Realists

The Great Realists

As we have seen, the North and Northwest of Germany were the regions most receptive to International Gothic; but they were also the regions that added the least to this style by way of change and further development. In the Southwest, on the other hand, the style of the day was combined with a sound and indestructible substrate. This sturdy trunk was able to slough off, without suffering harm, the branches that had been grafted to it, when these wore out, so to speak, about 1430. On the contrary, it now began to display an unprecedented vigour. This vigour was applied to the element of three-dimensionality and, in direct consequence, to the element of space. We are tempted to subsume this three-dimensional element under the heading of the elaboration of realistic detail so ubiquitously encountered in the art of the fourteenth and early fifteenth centuries, to see in it no more than a continuation and expansion of what was already under way. Actually, we come upon something fundamentally different here. First of all, there is a purely quantitative plus, for the fusion of space and three-dimensionality achieves a degree of verisimilitude that simply did not exist before. Even more important, however, is a qualitative difference, for figures seen in full depth turned out to become a force that could not but dominate the picture. Realistic elaboration of peripheral elements was still compatible with the flat, decorative style of yore, but this became quite impossible when the figures stood fully moulded in space. They now needed the picture space to live and move in. The picture became an analogy of something actually experienced. The beholder takes up his abode in it. In artistic terms, a scene painted around 1400 had still been a pattern of decorative relationships; but a scene painted by Multscher or Witz, by contrast, has become a segment of reality. Whatever the nuances of realistic fidelity, they all operate within this categorical approach.

Nor is it any accident that painting done in this new spirit now begins to emerge from the shadows of anonymity, that the outstanding protagonists of this new approach proudly identify themselves as the creators of their major works. This is as true of Lucas Moser's *Altarpiece of the Magdalen* in Tiefenbronn as it is of Hans Multscher's so-called *Wurzach Altarpiece* and Conrad Witz's *Altarpiece of St Peter* for Geneva Cathedral. All three of these painters were Swabian; and this region, which had long lingered in the wings of German painting, now, in the second quarter of the fifteenth century, not only emerged into full daylight but took on a role of leadership. Certain external circumstances had a part in this process—we have only to think of the Councils of Constance and Basel, which met interminably over many years and greatly stimulated art life along the Upper Rhine and in the

Lucas Moser (traceable 1409-1449).

Altarpiece of the Magdalen, dated 1431. Overall View with Closed Wings. (9 ft 10 in.×7 ft 10 in. with frame)

Parish Church, Tiefenbronn, near Pforzheim.

area fringing Lake Constance. The triumph of realism and individualization did away with the stylistic unity that had been an essential trait of art throughout Europe about 1400. In his fine book, *Die Anfänge der Tafelmalerei*, Wilhelm Worringer devotes illuminating thoughts to this phenomenon and its interpretation. "What dates from this time," he writes, "cannot be called a new style. Already another element is far too alive, an element precluding the genesis of any major style convention—the element of naturalism. Its triumph meant an end to the kind of internationalism that stood above character rather than being part of it. So long as painters saw with an inward eye, they could pay obeisance to style. Now that they trusted their visual sense, all became new and unique."

Lucas Moser

The earliest of the three altarpieces mentioned is the one by Lucas Moser. It was finished in 1431 and remains today in the location for which it was meant and created, the east end of the south transept of the parish church at Tiefenbronn near Pforzheim. Virtually intact in its original form, it is in a notably excellent state of preservation. The first thing to draw attention is indeed its form, a large pointed arch enclosing a figure shrine behind two tall rectangular shutters. The reason for this unusual shape was discovered only ten years ago, when mural paintings of this same shape, dating back to about 1400, were laid bare on the east wall of the nave. Evidently the *Altarpiece of the Magdalen* was meant to fit into this scheme. The figure of the Magdalen inside the shrine, a carving done about 1520, together with the strut-work above, constitutes the only later addition to the altarpiece. It is flanked by large statuary figures of Sts Martha and Lazarus on the insides of the open shutters, but the altarpiece really displays its main aspect only when they are closed. Within the ogive above is shown the *Feast of Simon the Pharisee at Bethany*. Below, in three upright oblongs are scenes from the life of the Magdalen: left, with her sister Martha and brother Lazarus at sea; centre, the saints upon their arrival at Marseilles; right, the Magdalen's last communion in the Cathedral at Aix. A predella, flaring like a console, shows *Christ amid the Wise and Foolish Virgins*, two of whom bear the features of Martha and the Magdalen.

The three main pictures of the altarpiece—the sea voyage, the arrival and the Communion —are separated by the frames of the shutters; but these dividers, rather than delimiting three distinct picture areas, are superimposed upon a single, continuous space. The sea on which the small ship with the saints approaches laps the steps on which the same saints have settled down to sleep; and the wall against which they rest fronts the church where the Magdalen receives her final Communion. This unitary space constitutes the whole picture's boldest innovation, for it is certainly not dictated nor even suggested by the story with its three scenes distinct both in time and space. A powerful inward need must have constrained the painter to seek "unity of place" for the three incidents, one taking place at open sea, the other outdoors before the city wall, the third inside a church. The subtlety with which he solved this problem is truly admirable. Without impairing the integrity of the three locales, he allows them to blend gently, one into the other, to overlap, so to speak. All the realistic detail is subordinated to this new verisimilitude. None of it draws conspicuous attention to itself, all is part of the whole—the glittering wave ruffles of the sea, the deep shadows cast against the city wall by the figures and other elements in the centre picture, the weathered portal sculptures on the right, even the scattered still-life objects in the lunette above. The realistic pictorial unity is in no way impaired by the numerous slips in realism.

The realistic space becomes the stage for figures that have a life of their own, not the kind of stylized life that marked the Soft Style. Their dress, rich but quite lacking in modish elegance, covers sturdy and active bodies rather than the dainty frames of yore; and in this respect they are quite distinct from the massive, languid, unarticulated figures of the Bohemian

Lucas Moser (traceable 1409-1449).
The Voyage of the Saints (detail). Scene from the Altarpiece of the Magdalen, dated 1431.
Parish Church, Tiefenbronn, near Pforzheim.

Theodoric style. Moser's vigorous figures do more than merely pre-empt space—they render more space visible than they themselves occupy. It is this space-devouring corporeality that is the painter's special concern. He never weakens it by distracting side effects. This may indeed account for his lack of interest in enhanced expression and individualized features. The most expressive gestures are found, of all places, in the group of sleepers. They do not, in other words, subserve the story as such, nor do they project character and personality. Instead they underline the physical bulk of the figures. It is precisely this objective, existential element that invests the whole work with such a wonderful sense of tranquillity and clarity.

One might expect that the landscape background would share the realistic approach to the figure, but such is not the case. It is true that the sea voyage of the saints represents a complete innovation in German landscape painting, for it too is a dominant element in the picture rather than a mere incidental; but that still does not make it realistic, at least when it is seen as a whole. It is the details that are realistic, the crinkly waves, the ships, the distant shores with their towns, castles and crowds. In its dreamlike and visionary overall character, this landscape is closer to Albrecht Altdorfer's *Battle of Issus* than to Conrad Witz's *Miraculous Draught of Fishes* from his Geneva altarpiece. The curious, almost dreamlike mood stems chiefly from the light reflected from the wave crests and the remote inlets. (The sea, by the way, is painted on tin foil, a curious parallel to the *Ortenberg Altarpiece!*) This glowing light seems in turn to reflect the gleaming gilt ground above the horizon, which this painter was

74

Lucas Moser (traceable 1409-1449).
The Arrival of the Saints at Marseilles (detail). Scene from the Altarpiece of the Magdalen, dated 1431.
Parish Church, Tiefenbronn, near Pforzheim.

not yet prepared to forego, as did Witz fourteen years later in his Geneva seascape and as the art of book illumination in France had done since the beginning of the century. We see that in his approach to landscape Moser was not yet ready to take the crucial, final step away from tradition, a step he had already taken so emphatically as a figure painter.

Who was this painter? Our most important source of information is the inscription on the right vertical frame moulding of the Tiefenbronn altarpiece: *lucas moser maler von wil maister dez werx*... This gives us his name and his ancestral home, the town of Weil der Stadt in Swabia. It is certain, however, that Moser did not have his workshop in this small imperial town but rather in powerful and art-loving Ulm. A Master Lucas is repeatedly mentioned in documents in that city, dating back to the period from 1409 to 1449, and one is tempted to relate these references to Lucas Moser. One of the donors of the *Tiefenbronn Altarpiece*, moreover, Wolf VI von Stein zu Steinegg, had close connections with Ulm. Lastly, there are certain local art works in Ulm that might be plausibly ascribed to Moser by stylistic analogy, especially the stained-glass windows of 1434 in the Besserer Chapel of Ulm Cathedral. Indeed, it has been suggested that Lucas Moser was primarily an artist in stained glass. If he flourished as early as 1409, he may well have worked in the region of Lake Constance during the time of the Council, which met from 1414 to 1418. This would convincingly explain his familiarity with ship-building revealed in the *Voyage of the Saints*; and the seascape itself might have been dredged up from his memory.

Lucas Moser's style certainly cannot be explained from the art of Ulm. We must view it against a much broader background. There are hints of Bohemia in it, and from Italy as well, and above all from French painting in International Gothic. Yet all these influences Moser made entirely his own. He did not so much "develop" them—in that event we should be still able to identify them, even in changed form—as appropriate them and recast them into his highly individual manner. Because of the unmistakably personal character of his *chef-d'œuvre*, these influences are easily overlooked.

Moser's individuality, by the way, is manifested even beyond the realm of art, in the famous words of the inscription on the left frame moulding: *schri kunst schri und klag dich ser din begert iecz niemen mer* (cry, art, cry, complain full sore, no one wants thee any more). It was the first time that an artist said something about his situation, and this outcry marks a new age in the history of art. It is true, of course, that the meaning of the inscription is not altogether clear. One may conjecture that in doing this work, a secondary altarpiece for a remote parish church, the artist was wistfully remembering the great challenges to art and artists that had been thrown down during the Council of Constance.

Hans Multscher

Since we are here dealing with German *painting*, the name of Hans Multscher should be really placed in quotation marks; for while we have much information about him and one of the most important pieces of evidence is his inscribed name on the painted wings of an altarpiece, we cannot be certain that he was indeed a *painter*. We do know that he came from Reichenhofen near Leutkirch in the Allgäu and that he was a *sculptor*. He is always mentioned in that capacity. He had a workshop in Ulm that was one of the busiest in that East Swabian city in the 1430's. He died in Ulm in 1467.

The problem of Multscher and his profession necessarily proceeds from his three works that are either signed or otherwise documented. Earliest of these are the sculptures of 1433 in the Karg votive niche in Ulm Cathedral, which bear the inscription: *Per me Johannem Multscheren... manu mea propria constructus* (made by me, Hans Multscher... by my own hand). Next come the wings (dated 1437) of an altarpiece whose other parts are lost. These reached Berlin from the Wolfegg Castle of Wurzach. The inscription reads: *bitte got fur hanssen muoltscheren... hant dz werk gemacht* (pray to God for Hans Multscher... who made this work). No mention here of "his own hand." Lastly, there is the completely preserved altarpiece —figure shrine and painted wings—from the Church of Our Lady in Sterzing in the Eisack Valley, today in the town hall of Sterzing (Vipiteno, near Bolzano). This work was commissioned in January 1456 from Multscher; and in July 1458 the master, accompanied by his assistants, escorted it to Sterzing, to finish the finer work on the spot. In January of the following year, Multscher was able to turn over the installed altarpiece to his patrons.

The sculptural portions of the *Sterzing Altarpiece* show, despite the lapse of time, the personal peculiarities of Multscher's sculptures dating back to the 1430's; but its painted wings are separated from those of the *Wurzach Altarpiece* by an unbridgeable gulf. We have had to conclude that Multscher cannot possibly have been the painter of the Sterzing wings. Whether the Wurzach panels are by his hand is an open question. It is not impossible that they are. In any event, this major specimen of German painting in the second quarter of the century remains closely linked with his name.

The two wings of the *Wurzach Altarpiece* were almost certainly not created for the castle chapel at Wurzach, but, according to Rudolf Verres, for the Hospital of the Holy Ghost in Memmingen. On one side they show four scenes from the Passion, in pairs, one above the

Hans Multscher (c. 1400-1467).

The Resurrection, dated 1437. (58¼×55″) Wing Panel of the Wurzach Altarpiece.

Gemäldegalerie, Staatliche Museen, Berlin-Dahlem.

(Wing panels reproduced in their entirety on page 151)

other: the *Agony in the Garden, Christ Before Pilate, Christ Carrying the Cross* and the *Resurrection*. On the verso are four scenes from the life of the Virgin: the *Adoration of the Newborn Child*, the *Adoration of the Magi*, the *Descent of the Holy Ghost* and the *Death of the Virgin*. Which of the two picture cycles was to be seen when the wings were open and which when they were closed can no longer be determined with certainty. What the theme of the lost central part was is wholly a matter of conjecture, but presumably there was a shrine with a group of carved figures.

In the individual pictures, the emphasis is strongly on the human figure and its three-dimensional impact. The last remnants of the obsession with melodious line are extirpated by the gravity and pathos of ponderous corporeality, of a kind never seen before. Umbra and penumbra, these two important adjuncts in projecting physical three-dimensionality, had already been introduced into painting by Lucas Moser; and in rational terms this meant the crucial step towards the new realism; but with Multscher something quite different is added: his figures are no longer marked by calm and tranquil serenity and discreet nobility—they are stalwart fellows and girls. In the words of Kurt Glaser, Christ is no longer the radiant Apollo of the new faith but rather resembles a village zealot. Christ is not actually carrying the cross, he is dragging it along, displaying an almost brutish air of helplessness. The Virgin in the two *Adorations* could scarcely be more peasantlike in aspect. Thus the physical realism of the figures is not dependent purely on technique and style, but is supported even by the choice of types. An added element is unusually vehement and exaggerated facial expression. This is not the outgrowth of a special interest in the variety and individuality of expression as such, which is instead placed entirely in the service of pictorial drama. Perhaps the most impressive example is the High Priest in the Pilate picture, ticking off Christ's bill of indictment on his fingers, his evil and pugnacious features, beside the irresolute mien of the Procurator, leaving no doubt how the issue will end.

Realistic space as a problem and goal in representation takes a back seat in the *Wurzach Altarpiece* to realistic figure. As in nearly all the pictures of the fourteenth century, space is created by a process akin to fitting together stage flats, and landscape is treated rather indifferently. In creating his interiors, the painter is usually content to use only a few props. In the *Christ Before Pilate*, for example, it is the canopy above the Procurator, symbolically suggesting the seat of power. Actually, this canopy is not attached to any consistent spatial structure. Outdoor spaces are encompassed by the expedient of physical limits of one kind or another. In the *Agony in the Garden* and the *Resurrection* there is no foreshortened perspective in the landscape backgrounds. Instead there is a tangible palisade or a board fence. Space of this kind, of course, can claim no greater realism than, say, the *Paradiesgärtlein* in Frankfurt. The schematically drawn trees and plants stand like points of reference in a pattern for a tapestry and suffer from the same handicaps. Occasionally this can lead to discrepancies, for example in the *Resurrection*, where the two sleeping guards seen from the back in the lower half of the picture look like cut-outs, because there is no space to respond to their emphatic physical realism, indeed, not even a real floor to support them.

This curious discrepancy between the treatment of figures and space is an important argument in favour of Multscher having painted the Wurzach wings. One would expect of a sculptor that he would give the figures absolute dominance, while relegating space to a mere relief background. A sculptor's approach is also revealed in the special manner in which space is objectified, by setting it tangible limits (compare, by way of contrast, Lucas Moser's shimmering space in his *Voyage of the Saints!*); and in a preference for compact, relief-like masses and groups of figures, as shown most impressively in the *Christ Carrying the Cross* in the *Wurzach Altarpiece*. Lastly, the conspicuous lack of interest in all subsidiary organic elements such as plants is something which at that time was quite to be expected in one who was a figure sculptor rather than a painter.

Hans Multscher (c. 1400-1467). Christ Carrying the Cross (detail), dated 1437. Wing Panel of the Wurzach Altarpiece.

Gemäldegalerie, Staatliche Museen, Berlin-Dahlem.

(Wing panels reproduced in their entirety on page 151)

The profound difference between the *Wurzach* and *Tiefenbronn Altarpieces*, in spite of their basically similar approach, is best explained on the premise that the one work is that of a sculptor who could paint, while the other is the work of a painter pure and simple. Beyond this difference, however, the two works are the expression of two different temperaments. It has been suggested that Multscher, coming from the Allgäu, the part of Swabia closest to the Alps, tended in his whole artistic nature more towards Bavaria than the West. Bavaria was the home of that vehemence and stalwartness that contrast so strongly with Lucas Moser's lyrical tranquillity. Passion, ostentatiously displayed, and a Bavarian peculiarity, is one of the clearest and most distinct regional characteristics of German art of the late Middle Ages. It remained visible throughout the fifteenth century, from the *Christ on the Cross* from the Church of St Augustine in Munich, by way of the Master of the Tegernsee Altarpiece, to Jan Polack.

It is no coincidence that the work of the painters who developed or flourished in the second quarter of the century is felt to be not only a pinnacle but also a turning-point. One would like to use the term crisis in describing it, in the literal Greek sense of "decision." It is in Multscher that we see with particular clarity that three-dimensional realism was far more than merely one of many possibilities, that this painter shook the foundations of painting and posed fundamental questions. A single example may serve to explain what is meant.

Hans Multscher (c. 1400-1467).

Christ Before Pilate, dated 1437. (58¼×55″) Wing Panel of the Wurzach Altarpiece.

Gemäldegalerie, Staatliche Museen, Berlin-Dahlem.

In the *Resurrection* picture of the *Wurzach Altarpiece*, Christ rises physically from the sealed sarcophagus. His left leg is still stuck in the stone lid, the crucial "seam" being but flimsily hidden beneath Christ's mantle. The Master of Wittingau allows the risen Christ to triumph plausibly over natural law and thus execute the miracle; but with Multscher an unresolved residue remains, an unbridgeable discrepancy arising from the realistic approach. This approach gets in the way of the transcendental and thus constitutes the definitive break with the Middle Ages; and here must have been the source of the effect of these pictures on contemporary viewers, an effect that literally shook them up. We begin to understand why from this point onwards further development was not consistent and undisputed. There was an immediate reaction; and the goal of realistic pictorial unity was to be attained only by a roundabout route and after incessant delay.

Conrad Witz

Conrad Witz, the most powerful creative spirit in German painting before Dürer—an "erratic block," in the words of Heinrich Wölfflin—was probably born in the early years of the fifteenth century in the West Swabian imperial town of Rottweil on the Neckar, but did his major work in Basel. Dürer always remained a clear-cut figure to posterity, while Witz had to be rescued from complete oblivion, by Daniel Burckhardt-Werthemann, about 1900. Here too a signature on an important work served as the chief source, an inscription on the frame of the *Geneva Altarpiece*, in which his name (Witz = wit) is literally translated into Latin: *hoc opus pinxit magister conradus sapientis de basilea MCCCCXLIIII* (Master Conrad Witz of Basel painted this work in 1444). The archives of the city of Basel give a good deal of information on the person of this Master Conrad Witz. In 1435 he swore the oath as a burgess, having been received into the painters' guild the year before. His wife was a niece of a respected painter, Nicklaus Rüsch, called Lawelin, who had lived in Basel since 1405, and with whom Witz, in what was later to become the Basel Armoury, executed a voluminous mural commission. By 1446 Witz is described as dead, or rather his wife as a widow. The painter's father, Hans Witz of Rottweil, figures as guardian of the five children. (Conrad has been variously identified as a namesake, known to have lived in Constance, and as the son of a "Hance de Constance," mentioned in Paris and Dijon. By this family tree, there would have been a direct connection with France and Burgundy; but the theory has not won converts.)

By stylistic comparison with the wings of the *Geneva Altarpiece*, authenticated as the work of Conrad Witz, it has proved possible to compile an œuvre of twenty pictures. Revealingly enough, all these attributions—for that is what they were—were accepted without a murmur. The evidence was completely persuasive, a rare case in art history. Nineteen of the twenty pictures are the remnants of three altarpieces; the last is a single panel, a *St Christopher* in Basel. Two other works, a *Crucifixion* in Berlin and a *Holy Family in a Church* in Naples, have always been controversial.

The earliest of the surviving groups is composed of the twelve pictures on the wings of the *Altarpiece of the Mirror of Salvation* in Basel, of which nine are in the museum at Basel, one in Berlin and two in Dijon. The inside pictures represent scenes from Jewish and pagan history, all of them so-called prefigurations of the events of the Gospel story to come. This prophetic system is detailed in the late medieval devotional book, *Speculum Humanae Salvationis* (the Mirror of Man's Salvation). Esther pleading with Ahasuerus, for example, prefigures the Virgin's intercession with Christ. The appearance of the three heroes before King David prefigures the Adoration of the Magi. Unfortunately, the whole pictorial programme of the altarpiece cannot be reconstructed, for the central panel and the predella with all the Christological scenes are lost. It is possible that shrine and predella consisted of carved figures. At least four of the wing pictures are also lost.

Conrad Witz (c. 1400-c. 1446).

Esther Pleading with Ahasuerus, c. 1434-1435. (33⅝×31¼″) Wing Scene of the Altarpiece of the Mirror of Salvation.
Öffentliche Kunstsammlung, Basel.

On the verso of the wings, an upper row of pictures comprising four panels showed an *Annunciation* (only the panel with the Angel is preserved) between symbolic representations of *Church* and *Synagogue*. Below these four panels there were presumably four large figures of standing saints and sibyls (only two of them, representing Sts Augustine and Bartholomew, survive). The *Altarpiece of the Mirror of Salvation* is undated, but it was doubtless done before the *Geneva Altarpiece*, which was completed in 1444. It is tempting and plausible

Conrad Witz (c. 1400-c. 1446). St Bartholomew, c. 1434-1435. (39⅛×27⅜″)
Wing Scene of the Altarpiece of the Mirror of Salvation. Öffentliche Kunstsammlung, Basel.

Conrad Witz (c. 1400-c. 1446).
The Annunciation, c. 1445. (61½×47¼") Wing Panel of an Altarpiece of the Virgin.
Germanisches Nationalmuseum, Nuremberg.

to believe that Witz moved to Basel in connection with the commission for the altarpiece, which would then have been done in 1434/35. The commission itself may indeed have arisen in connection with the Church Council, summoned to Basel in 1431. It has even been surmised that this altarpiece, probably intended for Augustinian canons of the Collegiate Church of St Leonhard, was meant to lend pictorial expression to the Council's main mission, reconciliation of the Eastern and Western Churches. One of the numerous efforts to reconstruct its themes and their sequence is based on this assumption. In any event, the *Altarpiece of the Mirror of Salvation* was an important and ambitious undertaking that had to pass muster before the critical and sophisticated eyes of the most powerful princes of the Church in the West assembled in Basel.

Conrad Witz (c. 1400-c. 1446).
Sts Joachim and Anne at the Golden Gate, c. 1445. (61⅜×47½") Wing Panel of an Altarpiece of the Virgin.
Öffentliche Kunstsammlung, Basel.

Witz must have stood the test, as shown by the commission for the *Geneva Altarpiece*, which apparently came to him during the life of the Council in Basel, at the hands of the Cardinal Bishop of Geneva, François de Mez. A one-time Chancellor of the Duchy of Burgundy, the Cardinal is likely to have had a discriminating taste in art matters, and the commission bespeaks the high prestige Witz had acquired among the participants in the Council. Created for the choir of the Cathedral of Saint-Pierre in Geneva, the altarpiece was installed on 20th February 1444. Whether it was actually done in Geneva or in Basel is a point that can no longer be settled; but the famous landscape depiction of the Lake of Geneva and the shore near the city in the *Miraculous Draught of Fishes* allows the conclusion that Witz must have sojourned in Geneva at least part of the time.

Of the *Geneva Altarpiece* too only the wings are preserved. On their insides, the two panels, wider than they are high, show an *Adoration of the Magi* and a *Virgin with a Donor Commended by St Peter*, both with gilt ground. The versos show the *Miraculous Draught of Fishes* and *St Peter Liberated from Prison*. We have not the slightest hint of what the central portion was like. It could as easily have consisted of carvings as of paintings.

Three panels in Strasbourg, Nuremberg and Basel must be looked upon as the remnants of a third altarpiece, on the theme of the Virgin, possibly from the Dominican Convent of St Magdalen in Basel. Two of them are shutter exteriors, a *Sts Magdalen and Catherine in a Church* and an *Annunciation*; the third is the obverse of the latter and shows *Sts Joachim and Anne at the Golden Gate*. This altarpiece must have been a late work, and we are inclined to place it in Witz's oeuvre partly before and partly after the *Geneva Altarpiece*.

The twenty surviving panels by Witz comprise a sequence of incomparable and unmistakable character. If we are entitled at all to speak of a personal style in the German painting of the Quattrocento before the advent of Pacher, it is here.

In attempting to characterize Conrad Witz, one must start with the pictorial role of his figures. Here lies the vital nerve of his art. The first thing to be said is that Witz isolates his figures, even when he combines several of them in a single composition. The exterior shutters of the *Altarpiece of the Mirror of Salvation* show only single figures—the two in the *Annunciation* are apportioned to two panels. The interiors comprise a pair of figures in each picture, but echoing the *Annunciation*, the four figures in the *Three Heroes Before King David* are divided, two to a panel, preserving the paired scheme. The three panels of the *Altarpiece of the Virgin* also carry two figures each. (From this aspect, the *Altarpiece of the Virgin* would have to be dated earlier rather than later than the *Geneva Altarpiece* with its many figures.) The principle of figure isolation, however, is honoured even in the panels from the *Geneva Altarpiece*, although they show scenes with many figures throughout. What this isolation means is that there are no compact, closed groups, as with Multscher, for example. Each figure retains its own *Lebensraum*, so to speak, even when it impinges on or overlaps another. The *Miraculous Draught of Fishes* may serve as a paradigm. The dominant figure of Christ stands quite free, and of the seven Disciples in the middleground only two actually overlap. The others are silhouetted, cut out, one might say. There are glimpses into the background between them.

The chief characteristic of the figures is their sculptural character. What seems to matter to Witz is their monumental and almost abstract moulding in depth, not their posture or expression or individualized features. He is not concerned with the supple and articulated "body" in the narrower sense, but with its three-dimensional bulk as such. In respect of anatomical grasp, Witz lags far behind Multscher. Beside Multscher's risen Christ, Witz's Antipater, baring his body in the *Altarpiece of the Mirror of Salvation*, seems almost doll-like. Yet in the whole of fifteenth-century German painting no figure can match his *St Bartholomew* in terms of rugged impact and inner firmness; and this painting has been rightly called one of the ancestors of Dürer's *Apostles*. The saint stands before us as though hewn of stone. (This sculptural character, by the way, was surprisingly confirmed in Hans Aulmann's studies of the *Altarpiece of the Mirror of Salvation*. Infra-red photographs revealed a preliminary drawing that seems almost chiselled. We are reminded of another preliminary drawing, by Conrad von Soest, for the *Wildungen Altarpiece* [see p. 49], so characteristic of the Soft Style in the gentle flow of its lines.) Hence the question arises whether Witz too may not have been a sculptor as well as a painter, as seems to have been true of Multscher. The advocates of this dual endowment are fond of citing an anecdotal poem written about 1470, in which there is mention of a painter named Witz, who lived in a town on the Rhine and was able to "paint as well as carve." Unfortunately this source is too poetic and imprecise to permit any firm conclusions in respect of our Conrad Witz.

Conrad Witz (c. 1400-c. 1446).

The Miraculous Draught of Fishes, 1444. (52×61″) Left Wing of the Geneva Altarpiece. Musée d'Art et d'Histoire, Geneva.

"Their being is their expression"—with these telling words Walter Ueberwasser has memorably captured the plausible though by no means realistic corporeality of Witz's figures. We would be indeed quite wrong to describe their wooden lack of articulation, their almost inanimate physical appearance, as a total absence of expression. They avoid the fidgety and exaggerated gesticulation that marked too much fifteenth-century German painting. Facial expression is restrained and never degenerates into grimace. Yet it is never weary. In the whole of late medieval German painting, the relation of man and woman was never shown more delicately, intensively and expressively than in those two widely differing panels by Witz, *Esther Pleading with Ahasuerus* and *Sts Joachim and Anne at the Golden Gate*.

Witz's attitude towards the problem of space must be seen in the light of his peculiar approach to figure painting. The *Altarpiece of the Mirror of Salvation*, when closed, presented the curious spectacle of a kind of honeycomb, in each cell of which a figure is placed. These bare and narrow boxes are not shown for their own sake, as a part of reality, a section of the world. They exist solely on behalf of the figures, concave counterparts to their convexity, so to speak. The walls of these compartments are primarily screens, against which shadows can be cast. This is seen quite characteristically in the later panel of *Sts Joachim and Anne at the Golden Gate*. As required by the story, the two figures stand outdoors before the city gate; but although the story does not require it, the gate is swinging open to form a kind of concave shell behind the figures. Most illuminating perhaps is the Nuremberg *Annunciation*. As always, the master places the two figures against corners of a bare chamber, seen from the side. He foregoes all furnishings, even such standard attributes as a prayer desk or a white lily, the symbol of virginal purity. In formal terms, this room has very little in common with the comfortable living-rooms in the manner of the Winterthur *Annunciation*, in terms of spirit and mood, nothing at all. This denial of the atmosphere of intimacy, this emphasis on the abstract quality of space precisely reflects the abstract physical quality of the figures, in whom liveliness of features is neglected.

Witz blends figure and space into a single unit. This is most conspicuous in the *Miraculous Draught of Fishes*, a true incunabulum of landscape painting and, as the first "landscape portrait," one of the most frequently cited and interpreted works of early German art. The achievement of the unity of space and figure was a historical event of great significance, although for the time being its impact was not widely felt. For unlike the contemporary Netherlandish painters, it stemmed, not from the steady, methodical and total conquest of visible reality, but from the unexampled subordination to certain laws of composition of a reality that was as yet by no means fully understood. It is only on this premise that we can begin to understand why a picture like the Nuremberg *Annunciation* is pervaded by an almost tangible sense of verisimilitude, even though it is far removed from valid realism in terms of perspective, lighting and anatomy. All the ambitions of the generation that succeeded Witz were pointed towards the full conquest of the real environment; and for a long time to come this could be achieved only at the expense of pictorial unity.

Just as Witz's artistic origins are obscure, so his succession is intangible, and this enhances his solitary genius. Witz certainly knew Netherlandish painting, especially the work of the somewhat older Master of Flémalle (Robert Campin), whose ponderous and massive figures are related to his own, and with whom he also shares a proclivity for vehement thrusts into space. The Basel painter has a rather lower affinity with the highly sophisticated Jan van Eyck, who was always after sublime effects—even though the "honeycomb" of the closed *Altarpiece of the Mirror of Salvation* always brings to mind the Ghent Altarpiece of Jan van Eyck. Could Witz have actually been trained in the Netherlands? The main argument against such an assumption is that he was unfamiliar with the enamel-like brush technique of the Netherlanders. He stuck to the German tradition of opaque tempera pigments. His debt to the Netherlanders is limited to certain elements. His basic creative principles are entirely his own. It is for that very reason that he was never able to give rise to anything like a "school" in Germany. Little of what came after him can be traced back to him. There is another reason for that, however. After mid-century German painting changed course and became enslaved to the Netherlandish school to such a degree that Witz's remoteness from that school became even clearer.

Divergent Trends
About Mid-Century

Divergent Trends About Mid-Century

THE works of the three Swabian painters, Moser, Multscher and Witz, are pervaded by a sense of grandeur and gravity without equal in German Quattrocento painting up to the time of Pacher and Dürer. They pinpoint the 1430's as a pinnacle in the development of art. The period that followed was strikingly characterized by Heinrich Wölfflin in these harsh and apodictic words: "The second half of the fifteenth century lacks character. The sense of simplicity and power was gone." The conquest of reality, ushered in by the generation born around 1400 but always subject to the severe discipline of art, was now driven forwards in all directions. The accent was sometimes on the colourful liveliness of the story, at other times on the isolated object. Now the spatial aspects of reality would be emphasized, and then again facial expression. The reality of experience, hitherto restrained by the filter of fixed systems of apperception, now threatened to overwhelm man, and in particular the artist's "sense of simplicity and power."

This trend was not confined to the art of Germany. It swept a much broader stage. We need only turn our eyes to the painting of Florence. Here too the monumental Masaccio, coeval with Witz, was followed by the graceful story-teller Fra Filippo Lippi and the magnificent Benozzo Gozzoli, with his pleasure in detail. In Germany the dispersion into various directions, quite different from the austere goals Witz's generation had set itself, was heralded while Witz was still alive. We may be reasonably sure, therefore, that the development of German painting after Witz, even as it appears to us in the light of a loss of individual power, nevertheless followed its own valid laws and retained an objective character that was rooted in the prevailing situation.

At first glance, the *Tucher Altarpiece* in the Church of Our Lady at Nuremberg still seems closely related to the Swabian realists. Probably done directly after the plague year of 1448 as a commission from the Tucher family, which still flourishes today, it originally stood in the Augustinian Hermit Church of St Vitus. It is a triptych, the central panel of which displays an *Annunciation*, a *Crucifixion* and a *Resurrection*. The open wings show *Sts Augustine and Monica* on the left, *Sts Paul and Anthony* as hermits on the right. The verso of the left wing shows a *St Vitus* and an *Assumption of the Virgin*, of the right wing a *Vision of St Augustine* and a *St Leonhard*. The central panel thus accommodates no fewer than three major scenes, in three narrow fields—there was no room to develop them in breadth, and they make do with a minimum of figures, which are still shown free-standing wherever possible. They

Nuremberg Master.
The Tucher Altarpiece, shortly after 1448. (6 ft 8 in.×17 ft 9 in.) Overall View with Open Wings.
Church of Our Lady (Frauenkirche), Nuremberg.

possess a physical weight and density that make them appear related to the figures of Moser and Witz. Other common characteristics are the restraint of their gestures and the simplicity of their contours. They are rather stocky in stature and pre-empt scarcely two-thirds of the total height. The upper termination is formed by a carved pelmet that extends across the full width of the altarpiece like a band of filigree, actually projecting before the gilt ground in the central panel, but punched into it in the wings. The gilt ground is drawn deep down, sparing only a narrow floor zone at the bottom. This serves only to enhance the silhouetted effect of the figures, crowded into their narrow fields. It is only owing to their powerful plasticity that they are nevertheless able to assert themselves rather than appearing as mere wisps. Their strong presence creates a kind of space of its own, to take the place of a space projected by illusionism.

It is not necessary to look only to Swabia for the sources and influences that gave rise to this powerful figurative idiom. Nuremberg itself had a rather different tradition leading precisely in this direction, the Bohemian style of Theodoric, which wrought its effect in the *Imhoff Altarpiece* about 1420 (see p. 47). This influence is unmistakably evident in the unique and characteristic relation between figures and space in the *Tucher Altarpiece*, the deliberate surrender of a clearly defined space. Once we have become aware of this deeper connection with the art of the Bohemian Court of about 1360, we are likely also to recognize in the absence of individualized features that baffling, fathomless quality that marks the heads on the wall panels of the Chapel of the Cross in Karlstein Castle and the figures in the votive picture of Jan Očko of Vlašim (cf. p. 28). Any inventory of qualities shared with the Theodoric style would, lastly, have to include the preference shown for subdued, almost dull colours.

This outrushing trend also gave scope for the full development of regional character to Southeast Germany, especially Upper Bavaria. We have already encountered the impassioned vehemence of the Bavarian temperament in the *Christ on the Cross* from the Augustinian church in Munich, done about 1390 (see p. 37, above). Throughout the fifteenth century the hallmarks of Bavarian painting were dramatic animation, bluntness, a propensity for extravagant form and a certain quality of crudeness. A striking example is the oeuvre of the Master of the Polling Altarpiece Panels. In his early period, especially the Virgin panels, dated 1439, in the Convent of Kremsmünster, he displays an almost morbid compulsion to invest the most ordinary motives with the character of caricature. Looking at the huge *tabula magna* of the high altar from Tegernsee, which dates from about 1445/46 and has given its name to a master once erroneously identified as Gabriel Mälesskircher, one feels at the mercy of a veritable witches' sabbath. Its *Christ Carrying the Cross* and *Crucifixion* teem with contorted figures. During the Baroque Age the latter picture was given a dramatic doomsday sky instead of what must have originally been a neutral background; and the fact that even this failed to destroy its pictorial unity is highly illuminating. One is tempted to apply the term "Proto-Baroque" to the work of this extraordinary master, and perhaps also to the most representative and stately *Crucifixion*, also from the Tegernsee monastery, in the Alte Pinakothek at Munich, a great panel fitted into a painted architectural framework. This device suggests it was part of an altarpiece

Master of the Tegernsee Tabula Magna.
The Crucifixion, c. 1450. (73×116″) Alte Pinakothek, Munich.

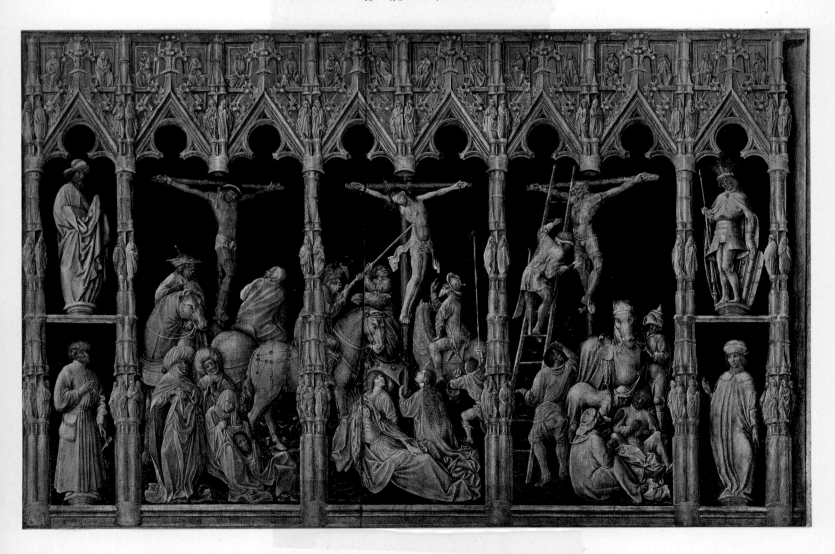

placed before a gallery in the church, with which it was meant to harmonize. The "animated" architecture in this work, together with the contrariwise "petrified" figures (a large number of them), results in an effect of alienation that points ahead at least to Mannerism, if not to the Baroque itself. Another unwonted quality in fifteenth-century painting is the effective device of working from the dark into the light, which we have already seen, in a less developed stage, in the *Christ on the Cross* from the Augustinian church in Munich.

This explosive and passionate quality recedes, becoming mere pepper-and-salt, as we move southeastwards and cross the borders of present-day Austria. The most important painter of this region was Conrad Laib, of Salzburg. Most remarkable among his works are two *Crucifixions*, one, dating from 1449, in Vienna, the other, from 1457, in Graz. They too are crammed with figures, making up a human wall that leaves virtually no square inch of space empty. At the same time this dense throng is totally lacking in dramatic animation. It is precious and intriguing detail that especially absorbs the attention of this painter. One senses that the Soft Style with its predilection for the exquisite lingered longer here than elsewhere. All the same, we can scarcely absolve Laib of the fault of "abhorring a vacuum." Evidently it was not in his nature to set accents in his pictures, to the end of creating a clear-cut structure, and he no longer commanded the sure decorative sense of the masters of the first quarter of the century.

The business of toying with painted architecture that marks the gallery altarpiece from Tegernsee also characterizes the major Thuringian work of this period, the high altar of the Reglerkirche at Erfurt. Created soon after mid-century, it is an altarpiece with two pairs of wings. When the inner ones are closed and the outer ones stand open, four scenes from the Passion are shown, taking place behind an arcade. Thin columns, looking as though they were made of cast iron, "carry" a gallery, over the balustrade of which lean twenty-four prophets engaged in animated discussion. The two Passion scenes proper, a *Scourging of Christ* and a *Christ Crowned with Thorns*, are of a hitherto almost unexampled mordancy—indeed, they seem to revel in blood and brutality. Here too we are reminded of the Bavarian spirit, especially the Tegernsee *tabula magna*, although the *Erfurt Altarpiece* seems to have come into being quite independently of the painting of Southeast Germany. Pictorial organization by means of pseudo architecture looked back on a certain tradition in Erfurt itself, and some signs point to the possibility that the painter came from the region of the Middle Rhine. One factor to be considered is that until the secularization of the clerical principalities in 1805, Erfurt was politically part of faraway Mainz.

Before mid-century an important painter appeared along the Middle Rhine. From the present location of two altarpiece wings, he has been given the tag of Master of the Darmstadt Passion. In certain works, especially two associated panels, a *Trinity* and a *Virgin and Child*, both in Berlin, he attains a degree of inward and monumental grandeur that makes him appear akin to the Swabian realists. The correspondence turns out to be one of approach, however, rather than of technical means. The extraordinarily effective depth of his figures is the result, not of their bulk, but of an almost crystalline hardness, a characteristic that points to the West rather than the Swabian South. At a time when the general development of German painting, after about 1440, tended toward fussy segmentation, his capacity for giving austere and monumental order even to scenes of many figures deserves special emphasis. It is especially evident in the Passion panels at Darmstadt and in the large *Crucifixion* at Bad Orb.

Of Moser's and especially Witz's monumental approach few traces were now left, even in their own regions, the Upper Rhine and Swabia along Lake Constance. There have been attempts to identify a "School of Witz," but on this crucial point the paintings in question differ fundamentally from the art of the Basel painter. This is impressively evident in the work of the most important "follower" of Witz, the Master of 1445. In the Basel museum the panel that gave him his name, showing *Sts Paul and Anthony* as hermits, hangs directly next to the works of Conrad Witz, and thus the difference becomes particularly plain. True, the figures of the two hermits are of blocklike compactness, but they fall short of dominating the picture. They do, however, blend with the enchanting landscape into a single mood. The dramatic conquest of reality has here yielded to a poetic sojourn within reality. The viewer is challenged to let his eyes rove over the picture, delighting in its every detail.

Stefan Lochner

Stefan Lochner, by far the most important Cologne painter in the 1430's and 1440's, came from Meersburg, also on Lake Constance, the region of the Swabian realists. He can scarcely have been very much younger than Witz. His work shows not a trace of the Swabian character and constitutes one of the most astonishing cases of artistic assimilation—astonishing even if we grant that he may have moved downriver while still a very young man. It is almost certain that he got his art training after he left his homeland, possibly in the Netherlands. Yet even these Dutch influences were completely integrated with the "style" of his adopted home in Cologne. There is a dual significance to this fact, first, from the point of view of the subsequent development of German painting, which from about 1460 onwards succumbed for decades to the Netherlandish influence, without being able to oppose this influence with a character of its own; and then as a token of Cologne's special capacity for appropriating and utilizing foreign elements. There was to be a similar case near the end of the century, that of the Master of the St Bartholomew Altarpiece, who came to Cologne from Holland (see p. 132).

An incidental fact about Lochner is as typical of Cologne as it is untypical of Swabia. Although he undoubtedly enjoyed high repute and authority in the splendid, art-loving city of his choice, none of his major works is signed. His name is often mentioned in documents in the time from 1442 to the plague year 1451, in which he died. We know the name of his wife and we know also that after 1447 he was a member of the City Council. Yet we owe our ability to associate certain works with his name to the testimony of an artist from Upper Germany who was mindful of what an artist's personality meant, none less than Albrecht Dürer who noted, in his diary of his journey to the Netherlands in 1520/21, that he had arranged to have the *Altarpiece of the Patron Saints of Cologne* unlocked, *die maister Steffan zu Cöln gemacht hat*. Using this key work as a point of departure, it has proved possible to reconstruct an impressive although not very numerous œuvre. Within it great altarpieces are carefully counterbalanced by intimate devotional pictures.

Among the earliest of Lochner's works to survive is the *Altarpiece of the World Judgment*, the central panel of which has remained in Cologne, while the inside faces of the wings, showing the martyrdom of the twelve Apostles, are in the Staedelsches Kunstinstitut in Frankfurt, and the versos, with three saints each, in the Alte Pinakothek in Munich. The main work of the early 1440's, the *Altarpiece of the Patron Saints of Cologne*, was originally located in the Council Chapel, a place of the highest dignity and significance. In 1810 it was transferred to the then still unfinished Cathedral, where it stands today. The third major work is a panel dated 1447, in Darmstadt, carrying a *Presentation in the Temple*, at one time probably the central panel of an altarpiece. Among smaller works, in the nature of devotional pictures, the *Madonna of the Rose Arbour* in the museum at Cologne is rightly the most renowned. For a whole series of generations it has been the epitome of early German painting.

To reduce the special character of Lochner's art to the briefest compass, one would have to repeat what has already been said of Cologne painting at the turn of the century: it is an art of tranquil and contemplative serenity and detached solemnity. True, Lochner's idiom is no longer that of the Master of St Veronica. The example of the *Martyrdom of St John the*

Stefan Lochner (c. 1405-1451). Altarpiece of the Patron Saints of Cologne,

c. 1440. (9 ft 3 in. × 17 ft 1 in.) Overall View with Open Wings. Cologne Cathedral.

Stefan Lochner (c. 1405-1451). The Martyrdom of St John the Evangelist, c. 1435. (15¾×15¾″)
Wing Scene of the Altarpiece of the World Judgment. Staedelsches Kunstinstitut, Frankfurt.
(Inner sides of the wings reproduced in their entirety on page 151)

Evangelist shows that in terms of the concise rendition of postures and anatomical understanding Lochner was actually Witz's superior, while he was at least his equal in the observa-
tion of detail—witness the crumbling stucco of the furnace! (Here, however, as in the case of
St Veronica with the Sudarium, one is entitled to ask just how one is to envisage the configuration of the martyr's body hidden in the cauldron!) Yet the detail is treated with considerable
reserve and without any real joy in the conquest of reality. Everything is in the end subordinated to a decorative scheme. The artist seems to find his proper voice only in the splendid
figures on the right, which afford him the occasion to display material ostentation. Lochner's
development follows indeed this direction. The *Altarpiece of the Patron Saints,* with an
Adoration of the Magi in the centre, is a dazzling spectacle, an important affair of state,
translated to the religious sphere. The gilt ground is no longer "sky" but "status symbol,"
and as such an essential element.

Stefan Lochner (c. 1405-1451).

The Presentation in the Temple (detail), dated 1447. Hessisches Landesmuseum, Darmstadt.

(Entire panel reproduced on page 152)

Lochner is likely to be passed over by those who scan the fifteenth century—the long eve of the Renaissance—solely for intimations of the future, for achievement bespeaking progress, for bold forward thrusts. He is the classic case of creative grandeur beyond the topical and the timely. (Half a century later, Hans Holbein the Elder was to provide an equally impressive example.) One is tempted to call Lochner the Bonnard of the fifteenth century. His artistic ambition is pointed at formal and emotional pictorial unity that leaves no unresolved residue. Yet this does not by any means lead him to forego coming to grips with visible reality. It is only that whenever he does come to grips with it, it is never from a passionate inner compulsion, but rather from the aspect of decorative enrichment and within the limits of what can be integrated into a whole. This may serve to explain a phenomenon that seems puzzling at first sight: somehow Lochner manages to picture the real and the ideal side by side, the one never challenging the other.

Lochner had no real followers. The Westphalian Johann Koerbecke, who flourished in Coesfeld and Münster between 1432 and 1491, the year of his death, can scarcely be described as such, although he borrowed compositions from Lochner for his *Marienfeld Altarpiece*, probably done after 1450. He outlived Lochner by some forty years, even though the two men must have been born about the same time. If the Cologne master had any more than a surface influence on Koerbecke, this was soon replaced by the much more stylish impact of Netherlandish art.

The Incursion
of the Netherlandish Influence

The Incursion
of the Netherlandish Influence

As we have seen, Swabian realism, certainly the most "modern" achievement of German Quattrocento painting and a deep thrust into the future, proved unable to prevail, even in the region where it arose, let alone in West and North Germany. Artistic trends of a very different kind managed to assert themselves beside it, and it was these that gave such colourful variety to the time immediately following, the middle of the fifteenth century.

The art of painting actually got into a kind of crisis, the chief mark of which was a loss of unitary style. In a different way, one could speak of a loss of vigour. It is noteworthy, to say the least, that in the second half of the century the emphasis moved more and more away from painting towards sculpture. There were no figures among the painters to compare in creative power with Jörg Syrlin, Veit Stoss, and Tilman Riemenschneider. Michael Pacher, the only painter of towering stature before Dürer, was at the same time a wood-carver. Painting found another and perhaps even more dangerous rival in the graphic arts, of which the painters themselves gained control after 1460. Two of the most important, Martin Schongauer and the Master of the House Book, were far more original and influential in their role as engravers. Graphic art accorded with the specifically German liking for linear expression. It gave greater scope to the unconventional, the new and young, and through this medium artists were able to circumvent their growing frustration as painters, stemming not least from the strict guild rules. They could work as they pleased, without waiting for commissions.

To regain a measure of stylistic integrity came to be virtually a matter of survival for German painting after mid-century. Unfortunately the prerequisites and forces necessary for the development of a clear-cut style were lacking. Only in this way can the almost resistless willingness be explained, with which German painting succumbed to the Netherlandish incursion. Indeed, this incursion was virtually invited. At the same time exposure to Netherlandish art was nothing new at all—many German painters had cultivated it before; but men like Witz and Lochner had always been able to hold out their own character against the Netherlandish influence. They integrated it with their own art, Germanized it.

Witz's generation had taken its Netherlandish lead from the Master of Flémalle and Jan van Eyck, but significantly enough the Germans who now looked in that direction went not to the pioneers but to the next generation, chiefly to Rogier van der Weyden (about 1400 to 1464) and Dieric Bouts (about 1415 to 1475). The new idealism, achieved by realistic means, which the van Eyck generation had planted in the mansion of art as a kind of explosive, had its fuse disarmed by the followers, so to speak. It was made accessible to the common taste, almost, one might say, watered down. These works no longer outraged anyone, no longer challenged artists to come to grips with the problem of reality on their own. They were comprehensible and serviceable models.

Curiously enough, the Netherlandish incursion seems least incisive in Cologne, where it is tangible in physical terms rather than having to be decoded from the local output alone. About 1460 a citizen of Cologne, Goedart von dem Wasserfasse, commissioned a late *chef-d'œuvre* from Rogier van der Weyden for the local Church of St Columba, the so-called *St Columba Altarpiece*, now in the Alte Pinakothek at Munich. It is against the background of this work, physically present in the city and bound to have had an important influence on local art, that we must regard Cologne painting after 1460, and above all its chief exponent, the Master of the Life of the Virgin, anonymous like all the Cologne painters of the second half of the fifteenth century.

The name of this productive master derives from the eight panels of an *Altarpiece of the Virgin* from the Church of St Ursula in Cologne, all but one of which are now in Munich. Together with some further works, they are among the most important achievements of German painting in the 1460's.

The most conspicuous quality of these pictures of the Virgin is their splendour, their thoroughly aristocratic demeanour. The people in them are dressed in precious fabrics, the architectural motives are wrought as by a goldsmith, all the figures keep themselves under the most careful control. The woman in the *Birth of the Virgin* who is daintily testing the temperature of the bath water in the basin is no ordinary serving-maid, but a lady-in-waiting carefully drilled by the chamberlain. We may well linger over this picture as thoroughly representative. The large, wide chamber that does service as the scene of the birth is not really an interior at all, but merely an earthly precinct marked off from the "universe" by nothing more than drapes. A substantial portion of the picture area is given over to the gilt ground. It is not merely placed by default, as in Witz's *Sts Joachim and Anne at the Golden Gate*. (This demarcation from the "universe" is made even more plain in the *Annunciation* panel, where two pieces of furniture, like stage props set into the deep gilt-ground picture space, are connected by a wall-hanging to make a frame for the scene. The drape, however, is of gold brocade, and this once again opens the "chamber" to the gilt ground.) Despite its spaciousness, the spatial quality of the picture is quite vague and inarticulate. This is echoed in the approach to the figures, which do not displace space, as with Witz, but simply move within a pre-existing space. It is their mobility rather than their corporeality that gives them "reality." It is this (in addition to the types themselves) that the Master of the Life of the Virgin owes to the Netherlanders. (Alfred Stange theorizes that he must have studied under both Rogier van der Weyden and Dieric Bouts.) Yet the inner compulsion with which he at once combines this reach for reality with an altogether different tradition is typical of Cologne. In his way Lochner had done exactly the same thing; but this combination of the modern with the traditional, this bridge-building between different worlds and degrees of reality, is a difficult undertaking, especially sensitive to the qualities and personalities involved. In less inspired works it leads to almost painfully feeble and stereotyped compromises—one thinks of the *Madonna of the Rose Arbour* in Berlin, which has been ascribed both to the Master of the Life of the Virgin and the Master of the Lyversberg Passion —but in the best works of the former it gains the impact of a creative reinterpretation. Indeed, despite all the archaic features, one senses here a powerful force that might well have become a harbinger of the future. If it turned out otherwise, there are reasons against which the individual artist could not prevail. At the very least the Master of the Life of the Virgin may claim to have been one of the greatest stylists of German Quattrocento painting.

Master of the Life of the Virgin. The Birth of the Virgin (detail), c. 1460-1470.
Wing Panel of the Altarpiece of the Virgin from the Church of St Ursula, Cologne. Alte Pinakothek, Munich.

(Entire panel reproduced on page 152)

Despite its conservative orientation and its failure to contribute to the general development of art, Cologne painting from Lochner to the end of the century maintained great vitality and character, a fact that becomes evident as soon as one turns one's eyes to the North. The region that had produced leading creative figures in the decades around 1400 in Master Bertram, Conrad von Soest and Master Francke now sinks into mediocrity for a long time to come. (The sole outstanding personality, Bernt Notke of Lübeck, was in the main a sculptor—indeed, his profile as a painter is only vaguely discernible.) The great Netherlandish masters found an eager following here. A major exponent is Hinrik Funhof, who probably came from Westphalia but flourished in Hamburg. His most important surviving work are the *Legends of Saints* on four wing panels of the high altar of the Church of St John in Lüneburg. Their tall picture divisions and figures to match, their pointed vistas into the background and their preference for mannered, courtly airs bespeak their dependence on the late work of Dieric Bouts, especially the huge Justice panels from the Town Hall of Louvain, now in the Brussels museum, on which Funhof may actually have worked as an assistant. In his own work everything comes out cruder by several degrees, and all that is left of Bouts's fine pictorial management is a pale and faltering echo. There is scarcely a sign of innate vigour, and here too the Netherlandish model probably served as the saving grace.

In South Germany the Netherlandish floodtide after mid-century brought a radical artistic reorientation. Nothing throws a sharper light on this than the example of Multscher. We have seen his *Wurzach Altarpiece* of 1437 as a powerful work of realism, with an emphasis on the physical bodies which, in this case, is particularly expressive. Two decades later Multscher concluded an agreement in Innsbruck to do an altarpiece for the Church of Our Lady in Sterzing in the Eisack Valley of South Tyrol. This altarpiece was finished and installed in January of 1459. As was presumably the case with the *Wurzach Altarpiece*, this one too included carved figures, with only the wings painted. The carvings bear the unmistakable mark of Multscher, but the painted panels are entirely different from those in the *Wurzach Altarpiece*. The powerful, space-creating bodies have given way to slender, mobile figures that simply inhabit wide spaces. The relation of space and figure has been reversed. The urgent, impassioned grappling with reality has yielded to tasteful arrangement. The figure composition, in the words of Gerstenberg, is "clean and well-ordered, but lacking in temperament." They are words that do more than characterize merely one case and one master.

Augsburg, cosmopolitan town of financiers and trade with distant places, seems to have been particularly receptive to the message of Netherlandish painting in the 1450's—half a century later it was to become the entryway into Germany for the Italian Renaissance. It was not merely the artists who accepted the new strain, but their patrons as well, as betokened by the purchase, in 1455, of a Flemish panel for the Corpus Christi altarpiece of the second main church of Augsburg, the Church of Sts Ulrich and Afra.

This church still holds today the most important relics of the early Netherlandish influence in South Germany, two large, oblong panels, done probably in the mid-1450's by the Master of the Legend of St Ulrich, who derives his name from them. His dependence on specific and surviving models from the circle of Rogier van der Weyden is so striking that some have regarded him as a migratory painter of Netherlandish origin. Yet the "accent" he gives to the Flemish idiom is so unmistakably Upper German that there can be no doubt of his real antecedents. The two panels are 75 inches wide each, and they were most likely meant to grace a large hall in the Benedictine Convent of Sts Ulrich and Afra. Like Lucas Moser's *Tiefenbronn Altarpiece*, they both show a unitary space divided by architectural elements into three subdivisions, for as many scenes from the legend of the city's and church's patron saint. In the panel showing the saint's dream and his Miracle of the Fishes, the middle scene is set in a deep space outdoors, flanked on either side by open structures that shelter the other two scenes. The open-air scene, surmounted by a sky with fair-weather clouds, evidently goes

Hinrik Funhof (c. 1435-1484/85). Scenes of the Life of St John the Baptist, last quarter of the 15th century. (84×63″)
Wing Panel of the Lüneburg Altarpiece. Church of St John, Lüneburg.

Master of the Legend of St Ulrich.
Scenes from the Life of St Ulrich, c. 1455. (76¾×46″) Church of Sts Ulrich and Afra, Augsburg.

back to a Netherlandish formula, but compared with its models it is conceived in terms of physical depth rather than painterly atmosphere. This is true also of the figures, which are seen with a view to their firm three-dimensionality rather than their surface texture. Some of the heads are of portrait character. Some critics have endeavoured to identify the young man looking out from the centre as Martin Schongauer.

The Swabian Master of the Legend of St Ulrich may indeed be a bit cruder and coarser than his Flemish models, which amounts to no more than a general characteristic; but he is also graver, more monumental, less Epicurean, and here we choose to see his personal quality. No German painter of the mid-fifteenth century ever came closer to the grand spirit of Tuscan murals. It is when such grandeur and powerful individual character are lacking that the dependence on the Netherlands becomes indeed the mark of Cain. This applies to the Augsburg followers of the Master of the Legend of St Ulrich and to a great extent to South Germany generally. One can scarcely exempt even so impressive an achievement as the great high altar of the Tiefenbronn church, the *chef-d'œuvre* of the Ulm painter Hans Schüchlin, which was finished in 1469.

The Netherlandish idiom was "spoken" in Nuremberg as well after mid-century. The most important personality to become even reasonably tangible is Hans Pleydenwurff, who came from Bamberg and took out citizenship in Nuremberg in 1457. A direct line of workshop affiliation leads from him to Albrecht Dürer; for after Pleydenwurff's death in 1472 his assistant Michael Wolgemut took over the studio, and in 1486 the fifteen-year-old Dürer entered that studio as an apprentice. Pleydenwurff's most representative work is a large *Crucifixion* in the Alte Pinakothek at Munich. In contradistinction to the Master of the Legend of St Ulrich, the Nuremberg master shows himself to be concerned with intriguing detail,

Hans Pleydenwurff (c. 1420-1472).
The Crucifixion (detail), mid-15th century. Alte Pinakothek, Munich.

(Entire panel reproduced on page 153)

the substance of things, precious clothes and figures of cultivated demeanour. Conversely, he neglected the spatial aspects of the landscape motive, which rises like a backdrop behind the Crucifixion scene, placed at the extreme foreground, and which lies beneath a gilt sky. The event is detailed with a certain reserved sophistication, and also with great skill. There is scarcely a hint of any religious mission or creative passion. We are able to observe here how the Netherlandish stylistic formulas could provide a solid support upon which painters could fall back when their own impulses were weak or deserted them.

Pleydenwurff owes his high standing in the art history of the declining Middle Ages to his *Portrait of Count George of Löwenstein, Canon of Bamberg*, in the Germanisches Nationalmuseum in Nuremberg, certainly done before 1464, although it is undated. It originally formed a diptych with a *Christ as the Man of Sorrows*, which is now in the Basel museum. The former panel is the first German portrait in the modern sense. Those that went before really showed the sitter only as an impersonal dignitary rather than an individual. It is Pleydenwurff who first showed the man in his portrait. The Master of Flémalle and Jan van Eyck had indeed asserted this new significance of the portrait as early as around 1430. Their approach aimed primarily at the sensible presence of the sitter; and Pleydenwurff too, showing his Count in a fleeting pose as he looks up from his interrupted reading, relates himself to this purpose. The precious robe and the almost genrelike motive of the book with its casually arranged cover and the thumb stuck into the pages serve the projection of actual presence; but an altogether different order of reality is rendered manifest in the old man's pallid and translucent countenance, the reality of the spirit. Beyond any physical inventory of features, the painter here

Hans Pleydenwurff (c. 1420-1472).
Christ as the Man of Sorrows, before 1464. (12¼×9″)
Left Wing of a Diptych. Öffentliche Kunstsammlung, Basel.

Hans Pleydenwurff (c. 1420-1472). Portrait of Count George of Löwenstein, before 1464. (13⅜×9¾″) Right Wing of a Diptych. Germanisches Nationalmuseum, Nuremberg.

(?) Michael Wolgemut (1434-1519).

The Resurrection. (69¾×44⅛″) Wing of the Hof Altarpiece, finished in 1465. Alte Pinakothek, Munich.

reaches deep into the inner man. This was a step of vast significance, nor was its meaning lessened by the circumstance that the Löwenstein portrait formed part of a devotional picture, in other words because the sitter was not shown autonomously but, in medieval fashion, in a religious context, facing his Redeemer. A straight road leads from this painting to Tintoretto's and Rembrandt's spiritualized portraits of old men.

Michael Wolgemut, Pleydenwurff's assistant and successor as workshop head, may serve as an example that a fascination with the clear-cut Netherlandish style could seal the fate of talented young painters not particularly gifted with originality. It was a style that offered convenient formulas and thus prevented any genuine attack on challenging problems of art. An altarpiece for the Church of St Michael in Hof, Upper Franconia, issued from the Pleydenwurff workshop in 1465; and it has been contended that two of its panels, an *Agony in the Garden* and a *Resurrection*, both reminiscent of Dieric Bouts, are the youthful work of Wolgemut, which seems probable, although not certain beyond doubt. If it is true, these two paintings constitute the luminous and promising beginning of a voluminous œuvre that slipped more and more into dry stereotype. Indeed, Wolgemut's importance in art history rests less on his work as a painter and "altarpiece entrepreneur" than on the book illuminations he created together with Hans Pleydenwurff's son Wilhelm late in the century. This work exerted a crucial influence on the youthful Dürer, preparing drawings for his wood-cuts.

The Netherlandish Influence
Grows Homespun

The Netherlandish Influence
Grows Homespun

Although German painting was in thrall to the Netherlandish influence from the 1450's until deep into the century's final decade, there were certain limits to the degree to which the great model could be appropriated. In virtually no case need one be uncertain whether a given work is Netherlandish or German. Was there, then, a specific German character at that time? This must be disputed, for several reasons. Let it be said at the outset that there is a notable gradient between Netherlandish painting and German painting influenced by it. Not a single painter from Witz to Pacher measures up to Rogier or Bouts, and even the "common herd" of artists in Germany were not nearly as well skilled in craft and technique nor did they enjoy the same level of artistic and intellectual culture. More to the point is the fact that the Netherlandish influence was quite unevenly absorbed, displaying many different aspects that are hard to reduce to any common denominator deserving to be described as characteristically German.

At least, what common element there is lies outside the visual sphere. We are rather inclined to look to the sociological aspects and pick the bourgeois character of German art as its common mark. In Upper Germany, where even after mid-century painting had its major concentration and density, the cities gained more and more of a monopoly of art life; and it was precisely in the cities that political power was passing from the aristocracy and the church to the bourgeoisie. In addition to individual citizens of wealth, the municipal corporations themselves became the major art patrons; and in those towns where the guilds ruled, painters, wood-carvers and goldsmiths were often their own patrons as members of the town council. The finest expression of this new power and bourgeois self-assertion is seen in the great town churches that grew up everywhere in South Germany in the fifteenth century, rivalling the episcopal cathedrals of the High Middle Ages, indeed outstripping them.

Three different trends, seemingly incompatible, mark the specifically German bourgeois attitude to the interpretation of Netherlandish art, which, while not exactly courtly, retained an aristocratic spirit.

First and most plausible is a notable coarsening, a greater crudity of expression. To use a linguistic analogy, the language becomes stronger and is even laced with vulgarisms, replacing the carefully chosen vocabulary of the Flemish, their cultivated play upon words. On occasion the Germans revel immoderately both in emotionalism and caricature. Overall

Friedrich Herlin (c. 1425/30-1500).

The Women Donors, 1462. (72×25½″) Wing of the St George Altarpiece. Stadtmuseum, Nördlingen, near Augsburg.

this is not always on the minus side. The robust down-to-earth quality that is the most vigorous and visible heritage of the earlier Swabian realism has its positive sides, supplying the kind of meat that is often lacking in Dutch painting with its penchant for the mannered and insipid. The second trend runs diametrically opposite, so much so that it may be explicable only as a form of compensation. The parvenu bourgeoisie, suddenly shouldering a cultural mission, began to usurp the aristocratic way of life in order to reassure itself of its power, and sophistication became the fashion of the day. Young people dressed foppishly. A kind of pseudo style emerged in art, something we may well call *préciosité ridicule*. Things never got beneath the surface, utterly at variance with the true nobility of the visual culture of the Netherlands. Third and last—and here lay the hope of the future—comes an increasingly urgent demand for inwardness, the "challenge of soul culture," as Dvořák has put it. Foregoing all stereotype, art was to portray direct religious experience, subsuming reality under this heading. This is the road that led in theology from late scholastic formalism to Luther.

We shall in the following pages be able to single out only a few characteristic works for these three trends and attitudes, from the very large store of paintings that survive from the three decades between about 1460 and 1490. The wealth and diversity of the whole can be scarcely hinted at. Only the two artist personalities that tower above the mass of mediocrity will be treated at greater length, Martin Schongauer and the Master of the House Book.

The case of Friedrich Herlin of Nördlingen (about 1425/30-1500) is particularly interesting and illuminating. A Swabian, he stands closest to the realism of Conrad Witz. It is assumed today that he spent at least two sojourns in the Netherlands or the Lower Rhine country. The wings from the high altar of the town church of St George, now in the Nördlingen museum, must have been done after Herlin's first exposure to Netherlandish art, about 1462. Before tackling the faces of these wings, the painter paid another visit to the West. In Cologne he saw Rogier's *St Columba Altarpiece*, and he copied some of the detail almost slavishly, "remaining himself only in the measure that he was unable to follow his model," in the words of Kurt Martin. Henceforth he stuck to Netherlandish pictorial formulas, with variable consistency.

The finest tokens of surviving Swabian realism—impotent as it was—are the famous panel of the Women Donors from the *St George Altarpiece* in Nördlingen, and a view of the town of Rothenburg, a panel from the high altar of the Church of St James in Rothenburg, done in 1466; but the earlier regional style lacked the vigour to maintain itself against the Netherlandish influence and proved incapable of establishing an autonomous school. It is significant that the panel of the Women Donors, pendant to a group of Men Donors on the opposite side, becomes most effective when lifted out of its context and viewed by itself. (When closed, the altarpiece originally showed two rows, one above the other, of four panels each, the Women Donors being located at the extreme right in the lower row.) There is not even any real connection with the originally adjacent panel on the left, showing Sts Barbara and Dorothy, despite an effort at spatial continuity, by means of a continuous, tiled floor and a similar green damask hanging. The eight panels as a whole make up a wild medley of outdoor segments and abruptly angled interiors, without consistent perspective. Yet the Women Donors by themselves are marked by a carefree naïveté and a sense of immediacy quite foreign to the Netherlands. The empirical linear perspective turns out to be a far more expressive device than it would have been, had it been technically correct, and the artlessly carpentered pews, without any pretence at illusionism, nevertheless evoke reality with rare power. The four women themselves impress as vivid personalities, even though they lack outright portrait character.

During the last quarter of the fifteenth century the animation and robustness of the pictorial idiom become more objective and externalized. It leans more and more heavily on features and gestures as the carriers of expression. At the same time there is a greater call for dramatic action.

A particularly impressive example is provided by four pictures from the obverse of the inner wings of the Augustinian Church of St Vitus, Nuremberg, today in the Germanisches Nationalmuseum. (In the older literature this work was confused and equated with Michael Wolgemut's *Peringsdorff Altarpiece*, owing to faulty reading of the sources.) The altarpiece from the St Vitus church is dated 1487. The four excellent pictures by the main master —a *Vision of St Bernard*, a *St Christopher*, a *St Luke Painting the Virgin* and a *Martyrdom of St Sebastian*—are noteworthy as a serious attempt to come to terms with the Netherlandish heritage. The wide, continuously developed landscape spaces are far more realistic than those from the Netherlands. In the *Vision of St Bernard* there is a small castle in the Franconian half-timbered style that is reflected in a lake. Ten years later, the young Dürer was to hark back to this motive, in his watercolour, the *House by the Pond*, now in the British Museum. The more dramatic scenes—the *Vision of St Bernard*, the *Martyrdom of St Sebastian*—bespeak a sense of inward agitation for which one looks in vain in the Netherlanders, as one does for the vigorous and richly contrasted palette.

In the Munich town painter Jan Polack, whose name hints at a Polish origin, this inward tension is enhanced to the level of savage agitation. Yet ever since the Master of the Polling Panels and the Master of the Tegernsee *tabula magna*, such baroque excesses and almost sadistically indulged scourgings and beatings were so common in Bavaria that we can scarcely speak of an alien element here. Opinion may vary on whether the mood this curious master portrays is genuine or not, but his numerous works (the most important of which were done in the time around 1490) are at the very least all of a piece and remarkably consistent. The bedlam of contorted visages and gestures is always echoed in the architectural and ornamental forms and even reinforced by the compositional scheme, as in the spiral movement of the *Ecce Homo* panel from the *Franciscan Altarpiece* in the Bayerisches Nationalmuseum. What we have here is, of course, more than a mere expressive coarsening of Netherlandish naturalism, which was Polack's point of departure as well. He rather proves himself a precursor of the strange Proto-Baroque, represented, for example, by Jan Gossaert and the Breisach High Altar towards the end of the Renaissance in the North. Yet Polack's significance in the development of art should not lead us to overestimate him. Rather than a true creator during the restless decades at the eve of the Reformation, he served as their passive expression. This is indeed true not only of Polack but for the bulk of German painters in the final quarter-century.

The two traits of German painting in the declining Middle Ages that seem almost mutually exclusive—forthright expression and pseudo courtly manneredness—are abruptly blended in the work of the most important painter after Schongauer and Pacher, the Master of the House Book. This combination alone shows him to have been a figure of extraordinary scope, and it is small wonder that his mysterious personality has intrigued scholars more than any of his contemporaries.

Jan Polack (traceable 1480-1519).
Ecce Homo, dated 1492. (81×51″) Panel
of the Franciscan Altarpiece of Munich.
Bayerisches Nationalmuseum, Munich.

Master of the House Book

His makeshift name is derived from a famous "House Book" in the collection of the Princes of Waldburg-Wolfegg at Wolfegg Castle near Ravensburg. It is a curious compendium of technical drawings by a gunsmith and "military engineer," with marvellous pictures of planets that belong among the most precious early drawings of any kind. In the older literature the artist was designated "the Master of the Amsterdam Cabinet," since most of his engravings (of many of which no other specimen is known) are in the Rijksprentenkabinet at Amsterdam. Both of these designations will be seen to apply to his graphic work; and it is indeed his prints and his drawings that have established his fame and his place in art history. His ninety-odd engravings, all of them apparently printed in only a few specimens from a soft and easily worn-down metal, possibly tin, are of an incomparable silvery delicacy. Beside their poetic richness Schongauer's copper engravings seem almost conventional, homespun and impersonal.

The scene of this master's work has been established with a high degree of probability as the Middle Rhine region, to wit Mainz. There is good reason for assuming, however, that he originally came from Holland and is identical with the Utrecht artist Erhard Reuwich, known as an illustrator of books. If this is true, he anticipates the case of the Master of the St Bartholomew Altarpiece in Cologne, to which we shall turn further on.

At the heart of his work as a painter stand the *Altarpiece of the Passion* from Spires, done about 1480 or a bit earlier, the greater part of which is in the Augustinian museum at Freiburg; and the far-famed *Betrothal* picture, done somewhat later and now in the museum at Gotha. The *Altarpiece of the Passion*, here represented by the panel showing *Christ Before Caiaphas*, plainly displays two very different tendencies. On the one hand, the Netherlandish element is evident in the careful organization of the interiors with their central perspective and superbly managed lighting. On the other hand, we find gross exaggeration of gestures and whimsicality of features. The impression is one of barbarians making themselves at home in costly chambers. The *Betrothal* picture in Gotha, by contrast, described by Buchner as "the classic portrayal of two lovers in early German art," is the finest expression of the stylized way of life, then held in high esteem, as already noted, although perhaps not the most typical example, since the occasion depicted is on the informal side. Unusually large in format (45 by 31½ inches), it is totally lacking in a sense of intimacy. The dialogue between the two lovers loses itself in the pointed gestures of the hands. Their faces bespeak little more than a certain open-hearted grace on the part of the man and seemly modesty on the part of the woman. Rather than displaying any true individuality, they become social types, and this gives the picture an archaic air. Some twenty years earlier, Pleydenwurff had given us far deeper insight into his sitter, in his Löwenstein portrait.

Although the *Betrothal* picture by the Master of the House Book seems to portray a couple of the old aristocracy, it does give us some insight into the bourgeois propensity for courtly airs; but far more illuminating in this respect is an early work by Bartholomäus Zeitblom (1455/60 to about 1520/22) of Ulm, who came from Nördlingen and was married to a daughter of Friedrich Herlin. This consists of the wings of an altarpiece from the Castle Chapel of Kilchberg near Tübingen, showing large, full-length figures of saints. St Florian in armour, the patron saint who protects against fire, looks like a solid citizen in fancy dress. The contrast between his somewhat quixotic get-up and his wonderfully vivid and expressive head is carried into the painting itself, which displays varying degrees of realism. It is these pervasive discrepancies that stamp such panels as a true expression of the prevailing intellectual climate.

We find this inner insecurity in even more clear-cut form in the work of the Master of Freising Neustift, whom Alfred Stange describes as a representative of the courtly style. His *Beheading of St John the Baptist*, from the Premonstratensian convent near Freising

Master of the House Book (active last quarter of 15th century). Christ Before Caiaphas, before 1480. (51½×30″)
Left Panel of an Altarpiece of the Passion. Augustinian Museum, Freiburg im Breisgau.

Master of the House Book (active last quarter of 15th century).
The Betrothal, c. 1480. (45×31½″) Castle Museum, Gotha.

in Bavaria, probably done in the late 1480's, is a virtual inventory of affected postures. The repulsive executioner might almost be one of Erasmus Grasser's nimble morris dancers in Munich. The grotesque figures are echoed in the unparalleled contortions of the composition as a whole. There is neither grandeur nor true feeling in such painting; and it makes the "challenge of soul culture" all too comprehensible, as it does the demand for "greatness of form" (which Dürer was to find in Italy only a few years later).

A particular contribution to an understanding of this "courtly style" of bourgeois painting may be provided by a marvellous pair of wings showing an *Allegory on Life and Death*. They were probably painted around 1480 in the Lake Constance region and are now in the Germanisches Museum in Nuremberg. The right one of the two narrow panels shows an exquisitely dressed pair of lovers seated in a blooming countryside, of the kind often seen in Netherlandish miniatures. A rich garden gives on townscapes, crags capped with castles, and lakes

Bartholomäus Zeitblom (1455/60-c. 1520/22).

St Florian, late 15th century. (58×27¾″) Altar Panel from the Castle Chapel of Kilchberg, near Tübingen.

Württembergische Staatsgalerie, Stuttgart.

Master of Freising Neustift.
The Beheading of John the Baptist, c. 1490. (57×28½″) Germanisches Nationalmuseum, Nuremberg.

that lose themselves in the shimmering distance. Two nude children are at play in the foreground. On the left wing is a corresponding landscape, but this one is frozen and desolate, with fallen and leafless trees. An already decomposing corpse lies in the middle. The houses are gutted, the towns and fields flooded, the castles falling into ruin. Everything is presented in exquisite detail. In the face of death, ever-present in those days and a central theme in art as never before nor afterwards, the ceremonious elegance displayed in the Life panel becomes a symbol of vanity, of the fleeting character of all things. We may well ask whether this deeper meaning did not play at least a part in the "courtly style" of bourgeois painting during the final quarter of the fifteenth century.

Martin Schongauer

Like the Master of the House Book, Martin Schongauer of Colmar, the most influential German artist of the decades from 1460 to 1490, simultaneously displays several trends of late Gothic painting. The dominant impression his art conveys is one of serenity and intimacy; and this view has been widely held ever since the time of Romanticism, for Schongauer is among the masters whose image never faded through the centuries—he did not have to be rediscovered by modern art scholars. There is little action in his devotional pictures, but mood and feeling come over very strongly, and this is the crucial mark of his art. Amid the *fin-de-siècle* mannerism of those decades, it remains a phenomenon of great significance.

We must not overlook, however, that Schongauer too had his "courtly" side, most strongly expressed in several engravings showing martyrs in affected poses. Combined with his bland and tranquil temperament, such emphatic sophistication often gives a saccharine effect. We find today the perfumed elegance with which Schongauer surrounded the figure of Christ in his late engravings not merely strange—it actually makes us squirm.

A solid base for our knowledge of Schongauer is provided by his 116 signed engravings; and it is these, together with his drawings, that influenced and stimulated the generation that followed him—the generation of Dürer—far more enduringly than his paintings. Most of these have apparently been lost. Only the *Virgin in the Rose Arbour* in the Church of St Martin at Colmar and the mural painting of the *Last Judgment* in the Breisach Minster can be accounted as authentic beyond all doubt, although a number of smaller devotional pictures may be confidently given to Schongauer, on the basis of his engravings.

The major unanswered question relates to the generation to which he may have belonged. He is known to have died in Breisach on 2nd February 1491, but was he born about 1430 or only about 1452? There is substantial support for either of these two possibilities. Schongauer's drawings, however, are so similar to those of the young Dürer that they could well be ascribed to him, and for this reason we are disinclined to regard Schongauer as having been very much older than Dürer, who was born in 1471.

Despite its mutilated condition, the *Virgin in the Rose Arbour* of 1473 in Colmar (a mediocre copy in Boston gives us at least an idea of the picture's original shape) is one of the most admired works of early German painting. This admiration stems both from the majesty of the main figure and the sense of intimate involvement which the viewer experiences. This is the precise combination that sets the whole tone for religious art in the West. The first component points in artistic terms to the Netherlands, and it is true that Schongauer owed a debt to that country, especially to Rogier; but the second element is native in tradition. The rose arbour, enclosing a quiet and intimate space without any real extension, has the same mood-projecting and artistic function as in the *Madonna of the Strawberries* at Solothurn, done about 1420 (see p. 64, above). Schongauer here succeeded in achieving what German

Martin Schongauer (c. 1430 or 1452-1491).

Virgin in the Rose Arbour, 1473. (79×44″) Collegiate Church of Saint-Martin, Colmar.

Master of the Lake Constance Region. Allegory on Life and Death
(detail of the right panel of a house altarpiece), c. 1480. Germanisches Nationalmuseum, Nuremberg.

(Overall view of both panels on page 153)

painting in the second half of the fifteenth century had vainly striven for. He truly integrated the Netherlandish influence with German art, made it bear German fruit. The crucial qualities of character that made this possible seem in the first place to have lain outside the sphere of art—the capacity for pure feeling, strongly experienced, a propensity for the natural, qualities that had been largely lost and that were to be among those most valued in the religious upheaval of the Reformation. When it comes to the artistic sphere proper the corresponding qualities are simple "greatness of form," inhering in such a masterpiece as Schongauer's copper engraving, the *Virgin in the Courtyard*, and the unprecedented poignancy of his draughtsmanship, setting its mark upon the art of the future, right down to the end of the sixteenth century.

Sunset and Dawn

Sunset and Dawn

THE Middle Ages and the Modern Age collide sharply in the final decade before 1500 and the first few years afterwards. In 1493 the Imperial Crown of the Holy Roman Empire descended to Maximilian I of Hapsburg, a man of dual aspect whom history knows as the "Last of the Knights" and who was also a patron and protector of the arts, taking the most progressive artists into his service and pointing them chiefly in the direction of the "modern" idiom of the graphic arts. A year before he ascended the Imperial Throne, Christopher Columbus had "discovered" America in the service of the Spanish Crown and thus taken the first crucial step towards European world dominion. In 1498 the Portuguese navigator Vasco da Gama had reached India by sea. The narrow confines of European life were ripped open and the scope of experience vastly multiplied. The Modern Age had dawned.

The earliest stage in the sphere of art was a natural overlapping of the medieval with the modern, of the late Gothic with the Renaissance. This should not surprise us—the surprise would be if there were indeed a hard-and-fast dividing line. It is not so much the fact that Gothic art survived for some time that constitutes a noteworthy phenomenon—this need scarcely concern us—but rather the intriguing forms of late Gothic painting with their unmistakable *fin-de-siècle* traits. Instead of being a stage of tired and resigned serenity, this was a time of nervous alertness, of daring experimentation with subtle effects, in short, an artistic orientation one may describe as a form of aesthetic hedonism. Beside it the contemporary works of young Dürer are almost crude and rough-hewn in effect.

We are here no longer concerned with the generation of Hans Holbein the Elder (born about 1460/65) and above all Dürer (born in 1471), which turned its back on late Gothic formalism, putting true religious feeling to the fore, together with an authentic world outlook, all of which went far beyond the realistic detail familiar to the late Middle Ages. This period is discussed in the companion volume, *German Painting from Dürer to Holbein*. Its first protagonists, however, still belonged to the older generation, especially the Tyrolean, Michael Pacher, born about 1435, and Rueland Frueauf the Elder of Salzburg, born a few years later.

Both trends in German painting at the close of the Middle Ages have their points of concentration on the periphery of the German language area, the conservative in Cologne, centre of Northwest Germany, the progressive in Southeast Germany, in the immediate propinquity of Italy. The most important by far among the Cologne painters of the declining

Master of the St Bartholomew Altarpiece (c. 1455-after 1500).
St Bartholomew between Sts Agnes and Cecilia, after 1500. (50¾×63″) Central Panel of the St Bartholomew Altarpiece.
Alte Pinakothek, Munich.

fifteenth century, the Master of the St Bartholomew Altarpiece, actually came from Holland. We are inclined to view this as an expression of the extraordinarily unstable situation that prevailed rather than as a mere accident. With Dürer leadership was once again to revert to a central region of Germany.

Master of the St Bartholomew Altarpiece

The outstanding figure of the *fin-de-siècle* Gothic style in Cologne is the Master of the St Bartholomew Altarpiece. The great work from which he takes his name was originally in the Church of St Columba in Cologne, whence it entered the famous Boisserée Collection, reaching Munich in 1827. Together with several other works that came to the Alte Pinakothek from Cologne by the same route, it served the Romanticists as the epitome not merely of Cologne painting, but of early German painting generally. In the attribution of this altarpiece to Lucas van Leyden, the Boisserée brothers came close to the truth, at least in terms of locale; for a recently discovered Book of Hours with miniatures by the hand of the Master of the St Bartholomew Altarpiece has provided proof that he came from South Holland, having

Master of the St Bartholomew Altarpiece (c. 1455-after 1500). St Thomas Examining Christ's Wound, 1495-1500. (56⅜×41¾")
Central Panel of the St Thomas Altarpiece. Wallraf-Richartz Museum, Cologne.

worked either in Utrecht or Arnhem. In the course of time, however, he became a citizen of Cologne, as did Stefan Lochner, who came from the Lake Constance region, half a century earlier. The St Bartholomew Master demonstrates for the second time that the important art centre of Cologne possessed an extraordinary ability to assimilate outsiders.

Once again the character of the work of this master is dominated by a solemn sense of splendour. Under the ministrations of this spirit, even at this late stage the pressing impact of reality is polished to a jewel-like glitter that belies its proper realism. Yet this revelling in precious solemnity fails to carry ultimate conviction, for all artless naïveté has long since dropped away from it. It is too ostentatious, too wrapped up in its own unexampled subtlety. In his relation to reality, the Master of the St Bartholomew Altarpiece reveals an ambivalent nature. On the one hand, he pulls out all the registers of realistic documentation. On the other hand, he drives this realism *ad absurdum*, blending his many realistic details into a whole that is altogether unrealistic. We encountered this phenomenon once before, in Hans Multscher's *Resurrection* (see p. 78, above); but what there reflected a true conflict, capable of solution, now, around 1500, becomes an artistic device, indeed something that arouses a sense of shock. This, by the way, is the self-same antinomy employed by twentieth-century surrealism—the unnatural combination of individual motives rendered with exaggerated realism into a new reality of the imagination.

The St Bartholomew Master found hints in this direction in fifteenth-century Netherlandish painting. Perhaps the most important is the motive of painted sculpture, familiar ever since the days of Jan van Eyck; but the Cologne master goes a step further, for example in placing in a painted altar shrine figures conceived in living terms. This is seen in the *Descent from the Cross* in the Collection of the Earl of Halifax, which was done about 1500 and is clearly influenced by Rogier van der Weyden's version in Madrid.

Different in kind is the dialectic of reality in the *St Thomas Altarpiece* from the Charterhouse in Cologne, probably done between 1495 and 1500. Evidently the shock effect of assembling figures painted with the utmost realism into groups translated to the supernatural ambience of heaven was no longer strong enough for him. People had long since grown used to that kind of thing in the second half of the fifteenth century. He now resorted to more drastic means, presenting the two main figures in monstrously contorted postures, and above all showing the doubting Apostle examining Christ's wound with gruesome verisimilitude. The impact of the scene is further enhanced by the contrast with the four attending saints on either side of the Christ-Thomas group, who are rendered with incomparable delicacy in all their nobility.

In the eponymous late work of this master, done after the turn of the century, the *St Bartholomew Altarpiece* now in the Alte Pinakothek in Munich, this unvarnished character has become sublimated. Seven saints are lined up on a narrow walk before a hanging of gold brocade that reaches to the level of their eyes, on the central panel St Bartholomew between Sts Agnes and Cecilia (and the kneeling figure of the donor, uncovered beneath an old overpainting only in 1951), on the left wing Sts John the Evangelist and Margaret, on the right wing Sts James the Less and Christina. These seven great full-length figures move solely by the rules of rhythmical musicality. Yet their tangible presence is almost obtrusive, and they cast strong shadows, against the drapery before which they stand. An almost paper-thin line of landscape appears in the blue distance above this curtain, which seems to stand rather than hang. The whole composition, we feel, is designed to evoke a shock reaction—the abrupt stratification of emphatic materiality and remote haze, the unreal delimitation by means of the curtain, the contrast between delicate femininity and fear-inspiring monster (in the figure and attribute of St Margaret). The fine-drawn proportions are a further characteristic of this master and his obsession with trick effects. Both the weedy walk at the bottom and the

Younger Master of the Holy Kindred (active in Cologne 1480-1520).

Triptych with Sts Bruno, Barbara, Dorothy and Hugo, c. 1515. (15×13⅜″ and 5¼″) Wallraf-Richartz Museum, Cologne.

landscape strip above the curtain, so important to the total composition, occupy only about one-twentieth of the height each. The heads of the saints barely project above the curtain. All this creates extremes in the proportions, and it belongs, at the level of abstract sense perception, to the shock effects with which this master operates. It makes him appear in the light of an artist and a man who deliberately sought out borderline situations. The fact that his most important works were meant for the Cologne Charterhouse, which was a centre of mysticism, has given rise to conjecture that he was himself a Carthusian monk.

Other works created at the same time in Cologne share the general features of the *St Bartholomew Altarpiece*—its cultivated painterliness, its material realism, its revelling in the splendid and the precious, its predilection for the sublime, the solemn, the tranquil. But these are all the traits they do share. The main element that is missing is the almost foolhardy audacity of its creative vision. A painter like the enormously productive Younger Master of the Holy Kindred, a name derived from a picture of that description in the Wallraf-Richartz Museum in Cologne, makes the difference all the plainer, because this master employs the self-same compositional schemes. The wings of the *Altarpiece of the Circumcision* in the Alte Pinakothek at Munich, for example, show an array of saints at full-length, quite in accord with the *St Bartholomew Altarpiece*. Yet the whole thing remains slack and homespun. Among this master's most charming and ingratiating works is a small triptych, only 15 inches high, in the Cologne museum, the central panel showing the Virgin with the boy Jesus and St Dorothy, while the Carthusian saints, Bruno and Hugo, with the figures of the donors, pre-empt the wings, making it likely that this little jewel too was meant for the mystical circle at the Cologne Charterhouse. Done only about 1515, i.e. almost contemporaneously with Grünewald's *Isenheim Altarpiece* and Baldung's high altar in the Freiburg Minster, it seems

Master of the Legend of St Ursula (active in Cologne around 1500).
The Vision of St Ursula. (48½×45″) Canvas. Wallraf-Richartz Museum, Cologne.

at first glance to belong to a much earlier stage of development. The landscape background, detailed with the most loving care, forms a fitting frame for the world of the beyond and the paradisiacally transfigured divine creation that are reflected in the figures. The enchantingly rendered countryside shows that the master was intimately familiar with Netherlandish art of the mid-fifteenth century. It is highly significant that in the central panel of the *Altarpiece of the Seven Joys of Mary* the Master of the Holy Kindred harks back to the composition of Stefan Lochner's Darmstadt *Presentation in the Temple*, dated 1447.

Every one of the late Gothic artists of Cologne about 1500 fulfilled himself in his own way. We should be quite willing to credit the Master of the Legend of St Ursula with a capacity for acquiring the "modern" formal vocabulary of the Renaissance; but that would only have given rise to the kind of covert Gothic strain that marks the work of the Netherlandish Romanists. This master's most impressive work, the *Vision of St Ursula*, from an eponymous cycle of paintings that are today scattered—it happens to be painted on canvas, by the way— is distinguished by a space-creating composition of great boldness, in which the material realism that was already current in Cologne is hardened to three-dimensional firmness. Yet, as Stange puts it, "the transfiguring effect of the lighting seems to remove everything from the sway of causality." We perceive something here that applies quite generally to Gothic painting in Cologne at its very last stage. These artists were by no means ignorant of realistic techniques. The overall archaic character of their work stems from a deliberate creative will. Indeed, what we call *fin-de-siècle* Gothic certainly has its true centre in Cologne, even though this variant can also be identified elsewhere in Germany. There, however, it was almost everywhere hopelessly outstripped by the new earnestness with its insistence on inward as well as outward truth, as exemplified in particular by Dürer.

We should perhaps mention the Swabian Master of the Rohrdorf Altarpiece, an ingratiating narrator whose pretended naïveté does not quite ring true. In Southeast Germany, the Salzkammergut, the Master of Mondsee and some others represent this trend in curious fashion. His *Flight into Egypt* in the Österreichische Galerie at Vienna is of enchanting grace and marvellous purity of feeling. Against a patterned gilt ground stands a bare landscape set with meagre shrubs in the Quattrocento style, before which the Holy Family travels on

Master of Mondsee (Upper Austria).

The Flight into Egypt, late 15th century. (22½×17¾″) Österreichische Galerie, Vienna.

its way. Everything is oddly frozen and isolated. The Virgin's kerchief and Joseph's mantle flutter in a non-existent breeze, standing stiffly in the air. It seems almost inconceivable that such works could come into being in the immediate vicinity of Michael Pacher's high altar of the Church of St Wolfgang. That it was nevertheless possible is a sign of an age in transition.

Michael Pacher

Michael Pacher of the South Tyrol enters upon the stage of German art history early in the final quarter of the fifteenth century as perhaps the greatest innovator of all, albeit one quite outside the broad mainstream of German art and not at all of Dürer's stripe. This is evident from the fact that we know only religious works from his brush, done almost exclusively on commissions from the Church. Apparently he had no part in the emancipation of the middle class, which served to establish the Modern Age, and furthermore he never cultivated the graphic arts, which were specifically an art genre of that age. His achievement remained within the framework of late medieval tradition, of which he was the last exponent, elaborating the altarpiece to its richest level. Yet this achievement included an explosively new style of rendering the traditional themes, a style that came to him through the intermediary of Italy, although this has on occasion been vehemently denied on the German side.

Michael Pacher was born around 1435 in Bruneck (Brunico), where he is mentioned as a master after 1467, or possibly in Brixen (Bressanone), where his family owned a farmstead. He and his brother Friedrich (about whom there is some question) have many associations with the Augustinian Collegiate Church of Neustift near Brixen, of which Leonhard Pacher, possibly our master's uncle, was Provost from 1468 to 1483. Documents describe Michael Pacher invariably and exclusively as a painter; but we know today with certainty that he was also a wood-carver. He died in 1498 in Salzburg.

Three of Pacher's works are authenticated by documents: the shrine altarpiece in the old church of Gries near Bolzano, for which Pacher received the commission in 1471 (the wings, unfortunately, are lost); the completely and excellently preserved shrine altarpiece of the Pilgrim Church of St Wolfgang on the Wolfgangsee (Salzkammergut), commissioned in the same year and finished in 1481; and lastly the high altar of what was then the town parish church in Salzburg (today the Franciscan Church) commissioned in 1484, but completed only just after Pacher's death. Of his paintings at best four fragments of panels survive, the two most important of which are in the Österreichische Galerie in Vienna. To these expressly documented works numerous others must be added. In the first place there are a series of mural paintings in Tyrolean churches; then there are the panels of a *St Lawrence Altarpiece* in St Lorenzen in the Pustertal, presumably an early work; and finally comes one of his undisputed masterpieces, the *Altarpiece of the Church Fathers* from Neustift near Brixen.

Of all Pacher's works the high altar of St Wolfgang is certainly the most important, if not the most mature. Its importance derives not least from the fact that it is preserved completely intact (together with the most interesting contract covering its execution), and this carries particular weight in the case of our master, who was painter and wood-carver in one. Apart from this, the *St Wolfgang Altarpiece*, together with Veit Stoss's *Altarpiece of the Virgin* in Cracow and the high altar of Kefermarkt near Linz (both done in the 1480's), constitutes the finest solution to one of the main challenges that faced German art in the fifteenth century, the creation of a shrine altarpiece with movable wings. They represent the culmination and consummation in the development of this type. Three decades later, in his *Isenheim Altarpiece*, Grünewald merely sought new creative scope within the existing form, without developing it any further as such; and in the high altar of the Freiburg Minster, done at about the same time, Hans Baldung Grien already initiated a process of retrograde development.

Michael Pacher (c. 1435-1498). The St Wolfgang Altarpiece, finished in 1481. Overall View with Open Wings.
Pilgrim Church of St Wolfgang am Wolfgangsee (Salzkammergut).

The *St Wolfgang Altarpiece* displays its greatest diversity when both its pairs of wings are open, as shown in our illustration. The wings with their scenes from the *Life of the Virgin* flank a shrine showing the *Coronation of the Virgin* in wood-carvings. This dialogue between painting and sculpture is repeated on a smaller scale in the predella. The carvings in the shrine find their continuation in the strut-work above, the relative proportion between figures and ornamentation being reversed. A more important question concerns the overall relation of sculpture and painting in this work. In slightly oversimplified terms we might say that Pacher the sculptor thinks primarily in painterly terms, while Pacher the painter thinks primarily in sculptural terms. The Coronation scene inside the shrine is set against a fathomless although not at all articulated depth. It is not given expression in any one isolated, three-dimensional figure. The whole scene, in the words of Oskar Schürer, is a "quivering mass." Linear accents guide the eye. The scenes on the wings display a diametrically opposite character. The figure groups are shown in interiors constructed in the most painstaking perspective, while the figures themselves are invested with the most vivid three-dimensionality. A highly significant detail is the pillar in the *Presentation* (upper right), a plastic motive *par excellence*, here shown directly in front of the figures in the middle of the picture. The artist's evident goal, in this mutual approximation of sculpture and painting, was to achieve a degree of unity for this highly diversified work, at least in overall visual terms; and here Pacher was on the road that leads straight to Classicism. Another significant highlight is that while the *Isenheim Altarpiece*, done about 1515 by the "anti-Classicist" Grünewald, retained the duality of sculpture and painting, the coeval Freiburg high altar by Baldung, who came from the school of Dürer, forewent the carved central shrine and the strut-work in favour of a painted panel, another method of lending a sense of unity to a work of this kind.

Unity is indeed Pacher's guiding principle in every one of his pictorial creations. We can readily understand that unity in terms of decorative two-dimensionality was no longer appropriate at this time, for the projection of reality, as experienced by the senses, had long since prevailed, at least in part, i.e. in individual pictorial elements; and realistic detail could scarcely be subordinated to an overall scheme of flat decoration. Thus unity could be achieved only by a uniform degree of verisimilitude, and this is properly Pacher's achievement. It can be seen in every panel of the *St Wolfgang Altarpiece*. A good example is the *Visitation* on the inside of the left predella wing. The three large female figures are shown against a landscape consistently developed in depth, the scale being given with great precision by the ground tiles and the building from which St Elizabeth is emerging. These figures are sharply modelled and the space itself is anything but neutral—on the contrary, it can only be described as markedly "active." This is even more notable in the interior scenes. One is tempted to say that figures and space are precisely "in phase." There is still another way in which figures and landscape are blended. Their realism is not complete, but in both cases it is at exactly the same remove from complete illusionism. The element that completes the fusion is the lighting, which Pacher invariably mobilizes in the service of achieving pictorial unity.

Pacher's whole creative development underlines this as the heart of his approach, especially his second major work, the *Altarpiece of the Church Fathers*, the painted portions of which are preserved virtually in toto, in the Alte Pinakothek in Munich. Presumably done about 1483 for the Augustinian Collegiate Church of Neustift near Brixen, it was taken to Munich by Bavarian troops, when the Tyrol was seized in 1812. The surviving central panel and the two wings undoubtedly constitute the bulk of this work, only the predella, the strut-work and other elements of the plastic framing being unaccounted for. With the wings open, the altarpiece shows a magnificent sequence of the four Church Fathers of the Roman Church, Sts Jerome, Augustine, Gregory and Ambrose, two on the central panel, one each on the wings. The crucial innovation is that central panel and wings are joined in a single overall compositional scheme. The four great saintly figures are shown in painted niches, architecturally elaborated with carved canopies that take the place of a three-dimensional shrine

Michael Pacher (c. 1435-1498).

The Visitation. Left Predella Wing of the St Wolfgang Altarpiece, completed in 1481. (28×23¼″)

Pilgrim Church of St Wolfgang am Wolfgangsee (Salzkammergut).

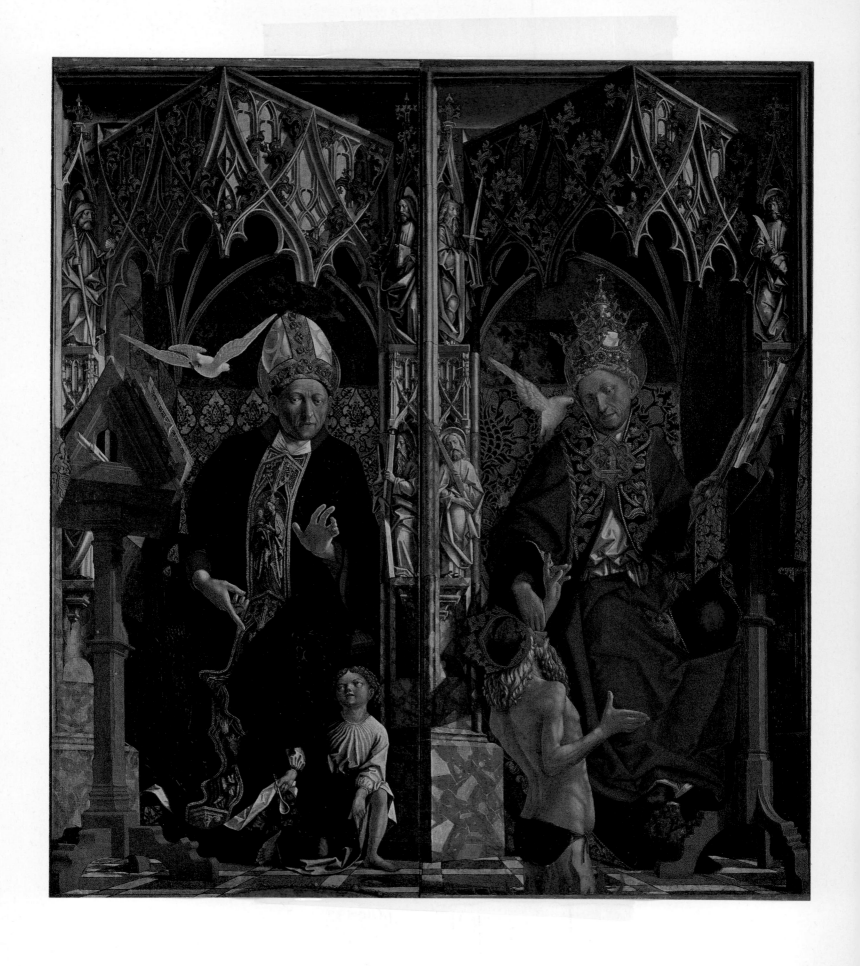

Michael Pacher (c. 1435-1498).
The Prayer of St Wolfgang, c. 1483. (40½×35¾″) Wing Panel of the Altarpiece of the Church Fathers.
Alte Pinakothek, Munich.

Michael Pacher (c. 1435-1498).
Sts Augustine and Gregory, c. 1483. (85×77″) Central Panel of the Altarpiece of the Church Fathers.
Alte Pinakothek, Munich.

More than that, central panel and wings form a single, continuous stage, its perspective constructed around a single, central vanishing point. The very low eye-level, aptly called "frog perspective," results in sharp foreshortenings, and this effect, underlined by appropriately chosen and placed objects—the lecterns in the central panel, the cradle on the right wing—again lends a markedly active character to the space. The three-dimensionality of the figures is no less emphatic. Generously proportioned, they are of an almost metallic hardness. The entire scene seems almost floodlighted, giving it a theatrical aspect and a highly stylized effect, despite its verisimilitude. This precisely calculated stylization holds the secret of the work's pictorial unity.

The four scenes from the life of St Wolfgang on the reverse of the wings of the *Altarpiece of the Church Fathers* are individual pictures. They share no single space, each scene having its own perspective. They serve as graphic examples of Pacher's impassioned struggle for new pictorial form, a concern unmatched by any German painter since Witz. In the *Prayer of St Wolfgang* all the pictorial elements are dramatically enhanced—the spatial construction with its low eye-level and knife-sharp foreshortenings, the contrast between indoors and outdoors, the almost palpable physical plasticity, the motive of the saint about to beat his head against the altar. Yet this dramatic quality is not merely on the surface, as for example in Polack's *Franciscan Altarpiece* in Munich, dating from the same time. It is not content with jerking the figures about like puppets on a string but achieves true pictorial integrity.

Nor is the magnitude of this achievement in any way lessened by our realization that it did not spring wholly from native soil. It is true that Pacher owes a considerable artistic debt to Tyrolean painting as a whole, and especially to the Master of Uttenheim, whom some regard as his teacher. That painter too displays the same sturdy, strapping figures and body, reflecting the bright southern light as though they were made of hard, lifeless material. There were, furthermore, clear-cut links between Pacher and the art of South Germany, especially the Upper Rhine region. We do not know whether he actually visited those parts during his journeyman years or whether the contact was by way of the engravings of the Master of the E.S. Monogram. The crucial influence, nevertheless, that shaped Pacher's art came from Upper Italy, and it is the work of Andrea Mantegna that must have left a particularly deep mark on him—his murals in the Eremitani Chapel at Padua, begun soon before mid-century, and the frescoes in the Camera degli Sposi in the Ducal Palace at Mantua, completed in 1474. Mantegna's architectural and decorative forms, harking back to antiquity, must certainly have startled the Tyrolean Pacher, child of the late Gothic Age; but these did not detain him—indeed, he all but ignored them. Nor, for that matter, are the tricks of perspective, the visual attack from below upwards and the audacious foreshortenings, at the heart of Pacher's Italian experience. The essential element is the new approach to configuration and pictorial unity. No precedent for this is to be found in German art in the second half of the fifteenth century, nor indeed in Dutch art. Pacher marks the point at which German painting turned from the West to the South. It was this new orientation that was to mark the next epoch, the time of Dürer.

Rueland Frueauf the Elder

Remarkably enough, another artist of Southeast Germany, Rueland Frueauf the Elder, anticipated the other great concern of German art in the time of the Reformation, sincerity of feeling, especially of religious sentiment, which somehow seemed then to have drained away from art as it had from the life of the Church. (Insofar as the abuses in the sale of indulgences were not politically and economically motivated, by the way, they corresponded precisely to this deterioration.) Frueauf, probably born about 1445/50 in Passau, was in the running for the commission for the high altar of the Salzburg parish church, but was compelled to give

Rueland Frueauf the Elder (1445/50-1507).

Christ as the Man of Sorrows, after 1491. (71¾×45¾") Back Wall of an Altar Shrine. Alte Pinakothek, Munich.

Rueland Frueauf the Elder (1445/50-1507).

Portrait of a Young Man, c. 1500. (7¼×6″) Österreichische Galerie, Vienna.

way to Pacher. His major works, of great significance in the development of art, date from the ensuing time. They comprise the panels with scenes from the Passion and the Life of the Virgin, dated 1490 and 1491 and now in Vienna, parts of a large Salzburg altarpiece, and above all the *Christ as the Man of Sorrows* in Munich and a portrait in Vienna.

The *Man of Sorrows* in the Alte Pinakothek, evidently painted on the back wall of an altar shrine, is among the most astonishing and moving works of early German painting. The simplicity, calm and purity of sentiment in this realistic work which foregoes all non-essentials are all but peerless. Though less concerned than Pacher with the problems of rendering visual reality, Frueauf shares his striving after three-dimensional form. The rigorous composition, with the dominant vertical of the Christ figure and the answering horizontal of the coffin, together with the numerous parallel lines, gives the picture an almost abstract character. All variety and vehemence are banished from the colour scheme. The whole picture breathes an utter tranquillity and a moving earnestness.

The significance of this new approach to portraiture is strikingly shown in the likeness of a youngish man in the Österreichische Galerie in Vienna. It achieves an unprecedented degree of immediacy, not by sharpness of detail, but quite the contrary, by foregoing it, together with all anecdotal elements or indeed anything that might detract from the main purpose. For the first time in German painting a sitter is here portrayed equally in his physical and his spiritual presence. Frueauf's masterpiece is the first fully "modern" portrait.

Thus Pacher and Frueauf, pursuing separate ways and doing different kinds of jobs, both reached their goal at the same time—the modern age, of which they were among the most important architects in the German sphere and in the sphere of painting.

Appendix

In view of the exquisite craftsmanship of so many early German panel paintings, it has sometimes seemed preferable to reproduce in colour a detail rather than the entire work. So that the reader may see these details in context, the relevant panels are reproduced in their entirety in the following appendix. In the case of three painters (Master Francke, Multscher and Lochner) a whole sequence of altar scenes is reproduced in order to give an idea of the scope and richness of these altarpieces.

Master Francke (traceable 1400-1425).
The Altarpiece of St Barbara, early 15th century. (5 ft 4 in.×17 ft) National Museum of Finland, Helsinki.

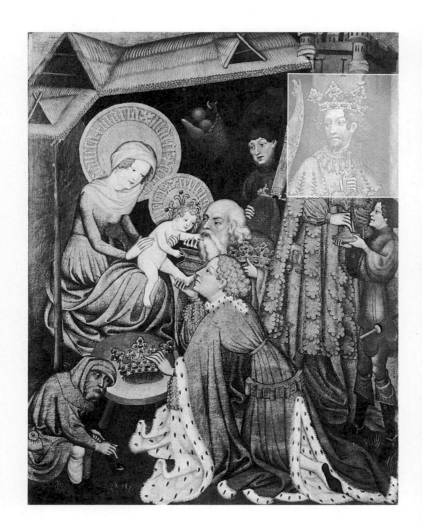

Middle Rhenish Master.
The Adoration of the Magi, c. 1420. Right Wing of the Ortenberg
Altarpiece. (39⅜×31⅞"). Hessisches Landesmuseum, Darmstadt.

Alsatian Master.
The Crucifixion, early 15th century. (48¾×33") Presumably from
the Church of St Martin, Colmar. Musée d'Unterlinden, Colmar.

Hans Multscher (c. 1400-1467). Wing Panels of the Wurzach Altarpiece, dated 1437.
(Each panel: 58¼×55″). Gemäldegalerie, Staatliches Museum, Berlin-Dahlem.

Stefan Lochner (c. 1405-1451). Inner Sides of the Wings of the Altarpiece
of the World Judgment, c. 1435. (Each scene: 15¾×15¾″) Staedelsches Kunstinstitut, Frankfurt.

Stefan Lochner (c. 1405-1451).
The Presentation in the Temple, dated 1447.
(54¾×49½″) Hessisches Landesmuseum, Darmstadt.

Master of the Life of the Virgin.
The Birth of the Virgin, c. 1460-1470. (33½×43″)
Wing Panel of the Altarpiece of the Virgin from the
Church of St Ursula, Cologne. Alte Pinakothek, Munich.

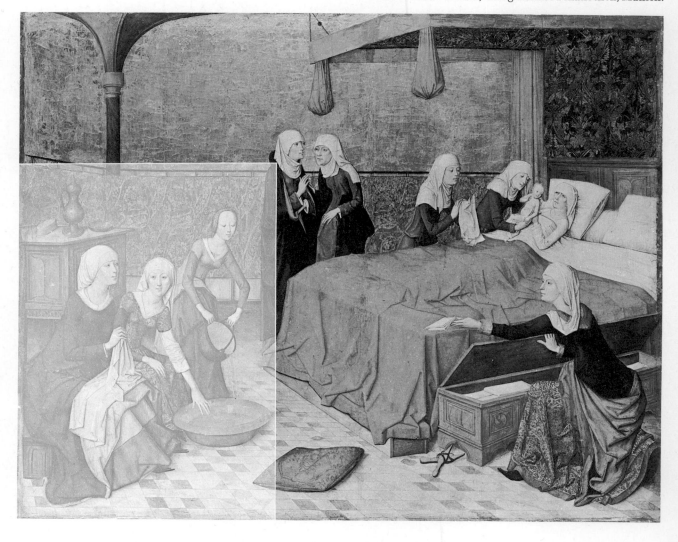

Hans Pleydenwurff (c. 1420-1472).
The Crucifixion, mid-15th century. (75½×71″)
Alte Pinakothek, Munich.

Master of the Lake Constance Region.
Allegory on Life and Death, c. 1480. Two Panels of a
House Altarpiece. (Each panel: 37½×8½″)
Germanisches Nationalmuseum, Nuremberg.

Select Bibliography

by

ELISABETH LANDOLT

GENERAL WORKS

Johannes von ALLESCH, *Das Raumerlebnis in der deutschen und italienischen Malerei am Ende des 15. Jahrhunderts*, in *Deutschland - Italien, Festschrift für Wilhelm Waetzoldt*, Berlin 1941, p. 3 ff. — Julius BÖHEIM, *Das Landschaftsgefühl des ausgehenden Mittelalters*, Beiträge zur Kulturgeschichte des Mittelalters und der Renaissance, Vol. 46, Leipzig and Berlin 1934. — Ernst BUCHNER, *Das deutsche Bildnis der Spätgotik und der frühen Dürerzeit*, Berlin 1955. — Idem, *Die Alte Pinakothek in München. Meisterwerke der Europäischen Malerei*, Munich 1957. — Fritz BURGER, Hermann SCHMITZ, Ignaz BETH, *Die deutsche Malerei vom ausgehenden Mittelalter bis zum Ende der Renaissance*, 3 vols., Berlin 1917-1919 (Handbuch der Kunstwissenschaft.) — Georg DEHIO, *Geschichte der deutschen Kunst*, Vol. 2, 4th edition, Berlin 1930. — Werner R. DEUSCH, *Deutsche Malerei des 13. und 14. Jahrhunderts*, Berlin 1940. — Idem, *Deutsche Malerei des 15. Jahrhunderts. Malerei der Spätgotik*, Berlin 1936. — Max DVORAK, *Kunstgeschichte als Geistesgeschichte*, Munich 1923. — Exhibition catalogue: *Europäische Kunst um 1400*, Vienna 1962. — Otto FISCHER, *Geschichte der deutschen Malerei*, Munich 1942. — Kurt GLASER, *Italienische Bildmotive in der altdeutschen Malerei*, Zeitschrift für bildende Kunst, new series 25, 1914, p. 145 ff. — Idem, *Die altdeutsche Malerei*, Munich 1924. — August GRISEBACH, *Die Kunst der deutschen Stämme und Landschaften*, Vienna 1946. — Barbara GRUND, *Probleme der Raumgestaltung in der Landschaftsdarstellung der deutschen Tafelmalerei vor Dürer* (Breslau thesis), Berlin 1934. — Peter HALM, *Deutsche Landschaftskunst des 15. und 16. Jahrhunderts*, in *Völkische Kultur*, 1934, p. 352 ff. — Max HASSE, *Der Flügelaltar* (Berlin thesis), Dresden 1941. — Arnold HAUSER, *Sozialgeschichte der Kunst und Literatur*, 2 vols., Munich 1953. — Ernst HEIDRICH, *Die altdeutsche Malerei*, new edition revised by Hans Möhle, Jena 1941. — Johan HUIZINGA, *The Waning of the Middle Ages*, London 1924. — *Katalog II. Alte Pinakothek München. Altdeutsche Malerei*, Munich 1963. — Karl Adolf KNAPPE, *"Um 1490". Zur Problematik der altdeutschen Kunst*, in *Festschrift Karl Oettinger*, Erlangen 1967, p. 303 ff. — Kuno MITTELSTÄDT, *Geburt der bürgerlichen Malerei in Deutschland*, in *Bildende Kunst*, 1957. — Heinrich MUSPER, *Gotische Malerei nördlich der Alpen*, Cologne 1961. — Walter PAATZ, *Verflechtungen in der Kunst der Spätgotik zwischen 1360 und 1530*, Heidelberg 1967. — Erwin PANOFSKY, *Imago Pietatis*, in *Festschrift für Max J. Friedländer*, Berlin 1927, p. 261 ff. — Otto PÄCHT, *Gestaltungsprinzipien der westlichen Malerei des 15. Jahrhunderts*, Kunstwissenschaftliche Forschungen, Vol. 2, Berlin 1933, p. 75 ff. — Idem, *Zur deutschen Bildauffassung der Spätgotik und Renaissance*, Alte und neue Kunst, Wiener kunstwissenschaftliche Blätter, Vol. 1, Vienna 1952, p. 70 ff. — Wilhelm PINDER, *Vom Wesen und Werden deutscher Formen*, Vol. 2: *Die Kunst der ersten Bürgerzeit bis zur Mitte des 15. Jahrhunderts*, Leipzig 1937; Vol. 3: *Die deutsche Kunst der Dürerzeit*, Leipzig 1940. — Grete RING, *A Century of French Painting. 1400-1500*, London 1949. — Alfred STANGE, *Deutsche Malerei der Gotik*, 11 vols., Munich and Berlin 1934-1961. — Idem, *Kritisches Verzeichnis der deutschen Tafelbilder vor Dürer*, Vol. 1: *Köln, Niederrhein, Westfalen, Hamburg, Lübeck und Niedersachsen*, Munich 1967. — Georg TROESCHER, *Kunst und Künstlerwanderungen in Mitteleuropa. 800-1800. Beiträge zur Kenntnis des deutsch-französisch-niederländischen Kunstaustauschs*, Vol. 1: *Deutsche Künstler in der französischen und niederländischen Kunst*, Baden Baden 1953; Vol. 2: *Französische und niederländische Kunst und Künstler in der Kunst Deutschlands, Österreichs und der deutschen Schweiz*, Baden Baden 1954. — Idem, *Burgundische Malerei. Maler und Malwerke um 1400*, Berlin 1966. — Friedrich WINKLER, *Sammelreferat zur Malerei des 15. und 16. Jahrhunderts*, Zeitschrift für Kunstgeschichte, Vol. 3, 1934, p. 204 ff. — Idem, *Altdeutsche Tafelmalerei*, Munich 1941. — Heinrich WÖLFFLIN, *Die Kunst Albrecht Dürers*, 6th edition, Munich 1943. — Idem, *Italien und das deutsche Formgefühl*, new edition, Munich 1964. — Wilhelm WORRINGER, *Die Anfänge der Tafelmalerei*, Leipzig 1924. — Idem, *Spätgotisches und expressionistisches Formsystem*, Wallraf-Richartz-Jahrbuch, Vol. 2, 1925, p. 1. ff.

REGIONAL SCHOOLS AND CENTRES

BOHEMIA

Max DVORAK, *Die Illuminatoren des Johann von Neumarkt*, Jahrbuch der kunsthistorischen Sammlungen des allerhöchsten Kaiserhauses, Vol. XXII, 1901, p. 35 ff. — Richard ERNST, *Beiträge zur Kenntnis der Tafelmalerei Böhmens, im XIV. und am Anfang des XV. Jahrhunderts, Forschungen zur Kunstgeschichte Böhmens*, Vol. VI, Prague 1912. — Berthold HAENDCKE, *Die Madonna in Königsberg/Pr. von etwa 1340 und der böhmische Einfluss*, Repertorium für Kunstwissenschaft, Vol. 46, 1925, p. 212 ff. — Antonin MATEJCEK and Jaroslav PESINA, *Gotische Malerei in Böhmen. Tafelmalerei 1350-1450*, Prague 1955. — Joseph NEUWIRTH, *Geschichte der bildenden Kunst in Böhmen*, Prague 1893. — Idem, *Mittelalterliche Wandgemälde und Tafelbilder der Burg Karlstein*, Forschungen zur Kunstgeschichte Böhmens, Vol. 1, Prague 1896. — Karl OETTINGER, *Neue Beiträge zur Kenntnis der böhmischen Malerei und Skulptur um die Wende des 14. Jahrhunderts*, Wiener Jahrbuch für Kunstgeschichte, Vol. 10, 1935, p. 5 ff. — Jaroslav PESINA, *Spätgotische Tafelmalerei in Böhmen*, Prague 1940. — Eberhard WIEGAND, *Die böhmischen Gnadenbilder* (Göttingen thesis), Würzburg 1936. — Idem, *Beiträge zur südostdeutschen Kunst um 1400*, Jahrbuch der preussischen Kunstsammlungen, Vol. 59, 1938, p. 67 ff.

COLOGNE

Harald BROCKMANN, *Die Spätzeit der Kölner Malerschule*, Bonn and Leipzig 1924. — Otto H. FÖRSTER, *Die Kölnische Malerei von Meister Wilhelm bis Stephan Lochner*, Cologne 1923. — Idem, *Das Wallraf-Richartz-Museum in Köln*, I, Cologne 1961. — Heribert REINERS, *Die Kölner Malerschule*, Mönchen-Gladbach 1925.

MIDDLE RHINE

Friedrich BACK, *Mittelrheinische Kunst*, Beiträge zur Geschichte der Malerei und Plastik im 14. und 15. Jahrhundert, Frankfurt am Main 1910. — Ernst BUCHNER, *Studien zur mittelrheinischen Malerei und Graphik der Spätgotik und Renaissance*, Münchner Jahrbuch der bildenden Kunst, Vol. IV, 1927, p. 229 ff.

NORTH AND NORTHWEST GERMANY

Hermann EHRENBERG, *Deutsche Malerei und Plastik von 1350-1450*, Neue Beiträge zu ihrer Kenntnis aus dem ehemaligen Deutschordensgebiet, Bonn and Leipzig 1920. — Carl Georg HEISE, *Norddeutsche Malerei*, Leipzig 1918.

NUREMBERG

Albrecht Dürer Exhibition, Germanisches Nationalmuseum, Nuremberg 1928. — Exhibition catalogue: *Nürnberger Malerei 1350-1450*, Nuremberg 1931. — Ernst BUCHNER, *Die Dürer-Ausstellung im Germanischen Museum Nürnberg*, Pantheon, Vol. I, 1928, p. 286 ff. — Eduard FLECHSIG, *Albrecht Dürer*, Vol. I, Berlin 1928. — Carl GEBHARDT, *Die Anfänge der Tafelmalerei in Nürnberg*, Strasbourg 1908. — Kurt PILZ, *Zur Geschichte der Altäre aus der Augustinerkirche St. Veit in Nürnberg*, Zeitschrift für bayrische Kirchengeschichte, Vol. 24, 1955, p. 150 ff. — Wilhelm SCHWEMMER, *Die Herkunft des Tucheraltares*, Anzeiger des Germanischen Nationalmuseums, 1936-1939, p. 118 ff. — Henry THODE, *Die Malerschule von Nürnberg im XIV. und XV. Jahrhundert in ihrer Entwicklung bis auf Dürer*, Frankfurt am Main 1891. —

E. Heinrich ZIMMERMANN, *Die Nürnberger Malerei der 2. Hälfte des 15. Jahrhunderts*, Anzeiger des Germanischen Nationalmuseums, 1932-1933, p. 43 ff.

UPPER RHINE, SWABIA AND SWITZERLAND

Julius BAUM, *Ulmer Kunst*, Stuttgart and Berlin 1911. — *Beiträge zur Geschichte der deutschen Kunst*, Vol. I: *Oberdeutsche Kunst der Spätgotik und Reformationszeit*, Augsburg 1924; Vol. II: *Augsburger Tafelmalerei der Spätgotik*, Augsburg 1928 (edited by Ernst BUCHNER and Karl FEUCHTMAYR.) — Bruno BUSHART, *Der Meister des Maulbronner Altars von 1432*, Münchner Jahrbuch der bildenden Kunst, 3rd series, Vol. VIII, 1957, p. 81 ff. — Idem, *Literaturbericht. Studien zur Altschwäbischen Malerei*, Zeitschrift für Kunstgeschichte, Vol. 22, 1959, p. 133 ff. — Idem, *Literaturbericht. Malerei und Graphik in Südwestdeutschland von 1300 bis 1550*, Zeitschrift für Kunstgeschichte, Vol. 27, 1964, p. 153 ff. — Lilli FISCHEL, *Die Karlsruher Passion und ihr Meister*, Karlsruhe 1952. — Paul Leonhard GANZ, *Die Malerei des Mittelalters und des XVI. Jahrhunderts in der Schweiz*, Basel 1950. — Hans HAUG, *L'Art en Alsace*, Arthaud, Paris and Grenoble 1962. — Werner NOACK, *"Weicher Stil" am Oberrhein. Stand und Aufgaben der Forschung*, in *Festschrift für Hans Jantzen*, Berlin 1951, p. 110 ff. — Hans ROTT, *Quellen und Forschungen zur südwestdeutschen und schweizerischen Kunstgeschichte im XV. und XVI. Jahrhundert*, 6 vols., Stuttgart 1933-1938. — Georg SCHMIDT and Anna Maria CETTO, *Schweizer Malerei und Zeichnung im 15. und 16. Jahrhundert*, Basel 1940. — Hans SCHNEIDER, *Beiträge zur Geschichte des niederländischen Einflusses auf die oberdeutsche Malerei und Graphik um 1460-1480*, Basel 1915.

BAVARIA AND AUSTRIA

Ludwig BALDASS, *Das Ende des weichen Stils in der österreichischen Tafelmalerei*, Pantheon, Vol. XIV, 1934, p. 373 ff. — Idem, *Malerei und Plastik um 1400 in Wien*, Wiener Jahrbuch für Kunstgeschichte, Vol. XV, 1953, p. 7 ff. — Otto BENESCH, *Zur altösterreichischen Tafelmalerei*, Jahrbuch der kunsthistorischen Sammlungen in Wien, new series, vol. II, 1928, p. 63 ff. — Idem, *Grenzprobleme der österreichischen Tafelmalerei*, Wallraf-Richartz-Jahrbuch, new series, Vol. I, 1930, p. 66 ff. — Ernst BUCHNER, *Eine Gruppe deutscher Tafelbilder vom Anfang des XV. Jahrhunderts*, in Beiträge zur Geschichte der deutschen Kunst, Vol. I, Augsburg 1924, p. 1 ff. — Idem, *Zur spätgotischen Malerei Regensburgs und Salzburgs*, Bayrische Akademie der Wissenschaften, Philosophisch-historische Klasse. Sitzungsberichte, 1959, Heft 6. — Alois ELSEN, *Gabriel Angler. Der Meister der "Pollinger Tafeln"*, Pantheon, Vol. XXVIII, 1941, p. 219 ff. — Walter HUGELSHOFER, *Eine Malerschule in Wien zu Anfang des 15. Jahrhunderts*, in Beiträge zur Geschichte der deutschen Kunst, Vol. I, Augsburg 1924, p. 21 ff. — Michael LEVEY, *National Gallery Catalogues. The German School*, London 1959, p. 7 ff. (on the London Trinity). — Vinzenz OBERHAMMER, *Der Altar von Schloss Tirol*, Innsbruck and Vienna 1948. — Karl OETTINGER, *Zur Malerei um 1400 in Österreich*, Jahrbuch der kunsthistorischen Sammlungen in Wien, new series, Vol. X, 1936, p. 59 ff. — Idem, *Zur Blütezeit der Münchener gotischen Malerei, I: Der Meister der Worcester Kreuztragung*, Zeitschrift des deutschen Vereins für Kunstwissenschaft, Vol. VII, 1940, p. 217 ff.; II: *Die Nachfolge des Worcester Meisters*, ibidem, VIII, 1941, p. 17 ff. — Idem, *Wiener Hofmaler um 1350-1380. Zur Entstehung des ersten deutschen Porträts*,

Zeitschrift für Kunstwissenschaft, Vol. VI, 1952, p. 137 ff. — Idem, *Ein österreichischer Porträts*, Zeitschrift für Kunstwissenschaft, Vol. VI, 1952, — Idem, *Ein österreischischer Kreuzigungsaltar gegen 1400*, Jahrbuch der kunsthistorischen Sammlungen in Wien, new series, Vol. XIV, 1953, p. 93 ff.

THURINGIA

Werner KLOOS, *Die Erfurter Tafelmalerei*, Berlin 1935.

WESTPHALIA AND HESSE

Hermann DECKERT, Robert FREYTAG, Kurt STEINBART, *Religiöse Kunst aus Hessen und Nassau, Kritischer Gesamtkatalog der Ausstellung Marburg 1928*, Marburg 1932. — Exhibition catalogue: *Westfälische Maler der Spätgotik. 1440-1490*, Münster 1952. — Exhibition catalogue: *Westfälische Malerei des 14. Jahrhunderts*, Münster 1964. — Käthe KLEIN, *Der Passionsaltar aus Osnabrück. Neues über den sog. "Laurentiusaltar" in Köln*, Wallraf-Richartz-Jahrbuch, new series, Vol. II/III, 1933-1934, p. 155 ff. — Werner MEYER-BARKHAUSEN, *Das Netzer Altarbild. Ein bisher unbeachtetes Meisterwerk der frühen deutschen Tafelmalerei*, Jahrbuch der preussischen Kunstsammlungen, Vol. 50, 1929, p. 233 ff. — Paul PIEPER, *Die altwestfälische Malerei, Forschungsbericht I*, Zeitschrift Westfalen, Vol. 27, 1948, p. 83 ff. — Idem, *Der Raum Westfalen. Das Westfälische in Malerei und Plastik*, Münster 1964.

MONOGRAPHS

Frueauf the Elder, Rueland: Ludwig BALDASS, *Die Kunst Rueland Frueaufs d. Ä.*, Pantheon, Vol. XVI, 1935, p. 227 ff. — Idem, *Conrad Laib und die beiden Rueland Frueauf*, Vienna 1946. — Ernst BUCHNER, *Ein Schmerzensmann von Rueland Frueauf dem Älteren*, Pantheon, Vol. XXXI, 1943, p. 73 ff.

Herlin, Friedrich: Julius BAUM, *Friedrich Herlin*, in Altschwäbische Kunst, Augsburg 1923, p. 31 ff. — Ernst BUCHNER, *Die Werke Friedrich Herlins*, Münchner Jahrbuch der bildenden Kunst, Vol. XIII, 1923, p. 1 ff. — Kurt MARTIN, *Ein unbekannter Altar von Friedrich Herlin und seine Herkunft*, Münchner Jahrbuch der bildenden Kunst, 3rd series, II, 1951, p. 89 ff. — Franz J. STADTLER, *Hans Multscher und seine Werkstatt*, Strasbourg 1907, p. 192 ff.

Laib, Conrad: Ludwig BALDASS, *Conrad Laib und die beiden Rueland Frueauf*, Vienna 1946.

Lochner, Stephan: Ludwig BALDASS, *Zur künstlerischen Entwicklung Stefan Lochners*, Wallraf-Richartz-Jahrbuch, new series, Vol. II/III, 1933-1934, p. 233 ff. — Lotte BRAND, *Stephan Lochners Hochaltar von St. Katharinen zu Köln*, Hamburg 1938. — Ernst BUCHNER, *Der Meister der Lindauer Beweinung und Stephan Lochner*, Wallraf-Richartz-Jahrbuch, new series, Vol. I, 1930, p. 100 ff. — Hans FELDBUSCH, *Stephan Lochners "Darbringung" im Hessischen Landesmuseum Darmstadt*, Das Münster, 2nd year, 1948-1949, p. 154 ff. — Otto FÖRSTER, *Stefan Lochner, ein Maler zu Köln*, new edition, Bonn 1952. — Andreas HUPPERTZ, *Stephan Lochners "Darbringung" im Hessischen Landesmuseum Darmstadt*, Zeitschrift für Kunstgeschichte, Vol. 15, 1952, p. 72 ff. — Kurt MARTIN, *Berichte der Staatlichen Kunstsammlungen*, Münchner Jahrbuch der bildenden Kunst, Vol. XIII, 1962, p. 250. — Helmut MAY, *Stefan Lochner. Der Dreikönigsaltar*, Berlin 1948 (Der Kunstbrief. 46.). — J. Heinrich SCHMIDT, *Zu Stefan Lochners farbiger Gestaltung*, Wallraf-Richartz-Jahrbuch, Vol. X, 1938, p. 132 ff. — Hubert SCHRADE, *Stephan Lochner*, Munich 1923. — Idem, *Lochneriana*, Wallraf-Richartz-Jahrbuch, Vol. V, 1928, p. 56 ff. — Alfred WOLTERS, *Lochners Apostelmartyrien im Städelschen Kunstinstitut*, Städel-Jahrbuch, Vol. IV, 1930, p. 100 ff. — Walter ZÜLCH, *Zu Stefan Lochner*, Pantheon, Vol. XXI, 1938, p. 155 ff.

Master of the St Bartholomew Altarpiece : Mechthild ANDREAE, *Der Bartholomäus-Meister, Gewandstudien zur Chronologie seiner Werke*, Innsbruck 1963 (unpublished thesis). — Rolf ANDREE, Helmut R. LEPPIEN, Horst VEY, *Nachlese der Ausstellung "Kölner Maler der Spätgotik"*, Wallraf-Richartz-Jahrbuch, Vol. XXIII, 1961, p. 327 ff. Frans BAUDOUIN, *Der Meister des Bartholomäusaltares und die südniederländische Malerei des 15. Jahrhunderts*, Wallraf-Richartz-Jahrbuch, Vol. XXIII, 1961, p. 353 ff. — K. G. BOON, *Der Meister des Bartholomäusaltares. Seine Herkunft und der Stil seiner Jugendwerke*, in *Kölner Maler des Spätgotik*, Cologne 1961, p. 13 ff. — Exhibition catalogue: *Kölner Maler der Spätgotik. 100 Jahre Wallraf-Richartz-Museum 1861-1961*, Cologne 1961. — Max J. FRIEDLÄNDER, *Neues über den Meister des Bartholomäus-Altars*, Wallraf-Richartz-Jahrbuch, Vol. IV, 1926-1927, p. 174 ff. — Eberhard HANFSTAENGL, *Die Restaurierung des Bartholomäus-Altares*, Die Kunst und das schöne Heim, Vol. 51, 1952-1953, p. 1 ff. — Paul PIEPER, *Miniaturen des Bartholomäus-Meisters*, Wallraf-Richartz-Jahrbuch, Vol. XV, 1953, p. 135 ff. — Idem, *Das Stundenbuch des Bartholomäus-Meisters*, Wallraf-Richartz-Jahrbuch, Vol. XXI, 1959, p. 97 ff. — Idem, *Der Meister des Bartholomäusaltares*, in *Kölner Maler der Spätgotik*, Cologne 1961, p. 21 ff. — Karl VOM RATH, *Der Meister des Bartholomäusaltares*, Bonn 1941. — Grete RING, *Die Gruppe der heiligen Agnes*, Oud Holland, 56th year, 1939, p. 26 ff. — Erich STEINGRÄBER, *Ein neu entdecktes Werk vom Meister des Bartholomäus-Altares*, Wallraf-Richartz-Jahrbuch, Vol. XXVI, 1964, p. 223 ff. — Rolf WALLRATH, *Der Thomas-Altar in Köln. Zur Ikonographie des Thomaswunders*, Wallraf-Richartz-Jahrbuch, Vol. XVII, 1955, p. 165 ff.

Master of St Veronica: Otto FÖRSTER, *Um den Meister der Veronika*, Wallraf-Richartz-Jahrbuch, Vol. XIX, 1956, p. 225 ff. — Paul PIEPER, *Die "Notgottes" im Landesmuseum Münster*, Zeitschrift Westfalen, Vol. 28, 1950, p. 182 ff. — Klaus Heinrich SCHWEITZER, *Der Veronikameister und sein Kreis. Studien zur kölnischen Kunst um 1400*, Würzburg 1935.

Master Bertram of Minden: Alexander DORNER, *Meister Bertram von Minden*, Berlin 1937. — Idem, *Der Passionsaltar von Meister Bertram in Hanno-*

ver, Pantheon, Vol. VIII, 1931, p. 401 ff. — Herbert von EINEM, *Das Problem der Herkunft des Hannoverschen Bertram-Altares*, Repertorium für Kunstwissenschaft, Vol. 52, 1931, p. 169 ff. — Adolph GOLDSCHMIDT, *Zwei Zeichnungen von Meister Bertram*, Jahrbuch für Kunstwissenschaft, 1924/25, p. 100 ff. — Viktor C. HABICHT, *Meister Bertram. Die Stilkritik und die Urkundenforschung*, Repertorium für Kunstwissenschaft, Vol. 52, 1931, p. 177 ff. — Hans HEUBACH, *Die Hamburger Malerei unter Meister Bertram und ihre Beziehungen zu Böhmen*, Jahrbuch des kunsthistorischen Instituts der k.k. Zentralkommission für Denkmalpflege, Vol. 10, 1916, p. 101 ff. — Jens Christian JENSEN, *Meister Bertram. Quellen und Untersuchungen*, Zeitschrift des Vereins für Hamburgische Geschichte, Vol. 44, 1958, p. 141 ff. — Alfred LICHTWARK, *Meister Bertram, tätig in Hamburg 1367-1415*, Hamburg 1905. — Friedrich Adolf MARTENS, *Meister Bertram. Herkunft, Werk und Wirken*, offprint of a Rostock thesis, Berlin 1936. — Paul PIEPER, *Miniaturen von Meister Bertram*, Jahrbuch der Hamburger Kunstsammlungen, Vol. 12, 1967, p. 35 ff. — Hans PLATTE, *Meister Bertram in der Hamburger Kunsthalle* (Bilderhefte der Hamburger Kunsthalle, I), n.d. — Idem, *Meister Bertram. Die Schöpfungsgeschichte*, Reclam, Stuttgart 1956. (Werkmonographien zur bildenden Kunst. 3.) — Paul PORTMANN, *Meister Bertram*, Zurich 1963. — Helga RENSING, *Studien zur Kunst Meister Bertrams von Minden*, thesis presented at Munich, 1952 (unpublished). — Alfred ROHDE, *Der Hamburger Petri-Altar des Meister Bertram von Minden*, Pantheon, Vol. XV, 1935, p. 154 ff. — Hubert STIERLING, *Theologische Erklärungen zu einigen Bildern Meister Bertrams in der Hamburger Kunsthalle*, Repertorium für Kunstwissenschaft, Vol. XLIV, 1924, p. 263 ff. — Georg Graf VITZTHUM, *Der Hochaltar der Jakobikirche in Göttingen*, Göttinger Beiträge zur deutschen Kunstgeschichte, Göttingen 1927, p. 53 ff.

Master of the Erfurt Altarpiece: Lilli FISCHEL, *Studien in der altdeutschen Abteilung der Badischen Kunsthalle. I. Neues über den Meister des Erfurter Regleraltars*, Oberrheinische Kunst, 6th year, 1934, p. 15 ff. — Walter HUGELSHOFER, *Ein Bild vom Meister des Erfurter Regler-Altars*, in *Beiträge zur Geschichte der deutschen Kunst*, Vol. I, Augsburg 1924, p. 58 ff.

Master Francke: Harald BROCKMANN, *Die Entwicklungslinie in der Kunst Meister Franckes*, Jahrbuch für Kunstwissenschaft, 1927, p. 1 ff. — Adolph GOLDSCHMIDT, *Ein Altarschrein Meister Franckes in Finnland*, Zeitschrift für bildende Kunst, Vol. XXVI, 1915, p. 17 ff. — Robert HERRLINGER, *Der Thomasaltar Meister Franckes und die deutsche Plastik des frühen 15. Jahrhunderts*, Zeitschrift für Kunst, Vol. 2, 1948, p. 230 ff. — Ottmar KERBER, *Meister Francke und die deutsche Kunst um 1400*, Part I: *Der Barbara Altar*, Kallmunz 1939. — Alfred LICHTWARK, *Meister Francke*, Hamburg 1899. — Bella MARTENS, *Meister Francke*, Hamburg 1929. — Herbert PEE, *Meister Francke. Der Englandfahrer-Altar*, Reclam, Stuttgart 1967. (Werkmonographien zur bildenden Kunst. 122.) — Heinrich REINCKE, *Probleme um den "Meister Francke"*, Jahrbuch der Hamburger Kunstsammlungen, Vol. 4, 1959, p. 9 ff. — Theodor RENSING, *Über die Herkunft des Meisters Francke*, Wallraf-Richartz-Jahrbuch, Vol. XXIX, 1967, p. 31 ff.

Master of Hohenfurth (or Master of Vyssi Brod): K. CHYTILL, *Das Madonnenbild des Prager Erzbischofs Ernst im Kaiser-Friedrich-Museum*, Jahrbuch der königl. Preussischen Kunstsammlungen, Vol. 28, 1907, p. 131 ff. — Werner R. DEUSCH, *Der Meister von Hohenfurt*, Kunst-Rundschau, 48th year, 1940, p. 87 ff. — Betty KURTH, *Das Gnadenbild als Stilvermittler*, Belvedere, Vol. 12, 1934, p. 6 ff.

Master of the House Book: Ludwig BALDASS, *Beiträge zur Hausbuchmeisterfrage*, Oberrheinische Kunst, 2nd year, 1926-1927, p. 182 ff. — Lottlisa BEHLING, *Der Hausbuchmeister. Erhard Rewich*, Zeitschrift für Kunstwissenschaft, Vol. V, p. 179 ff. — Idem, *Eine Hausbuchmeisterscheibe im Kölner Schnütgen-Museum*, in *Festschrift Friedrich Winkler*, Berlin 1959, p. 141 ff. — J.C.J. BIERENS DE HAAN, *De Meester van het Amsterdamsch Kabinet*, Amsterdam 1947. — Exhibition catalogue: *Deutsche Zeichnungen 1400-1900*, Munich 1955, p. 21 ff. — Walter HOTZ, *Der "Hausbuchmeister" Nikolaus Nievergalt und sein Kreis*, Der Wormsgau, Vol. 3, Heft 3, Worms 1953. — Ernstotto Graf ZU SOLMS-LAUBACH, *Der Hausbuchmeister*, Städel-Jahrbuch, Vol. 9, 1935-1936, p. 13 ff. — Idem, *Nachtrag zu Erhard Reuwich*, Zeitschrift für Kunstwissenschaft, Vol. 10, 1956, p. 187 ff. — Alfred STANGE, *Der Hausbuchmeister, Gesamtdarstellung und Katalog seiner Gemälde, Kupferstiche und Zeichnungen*, Baden-Baden and Strasbourg 1958. — Idem, *Untersuchungen über die Anfänge des Hausbuchmeisters*, Das Münster, 9th year, 1956, p. 381 ff. — Johannes Graf VON WALDBURG-WOLFEGG, *Das mittelalterliche Hausbuch*, Munich 1957. — Wolfgang WEGNER, *Mittelalterliche Kunst der nördlichen Niederlande, Die Jubiläumsausstellung des Rijksmuseums in Amsterdam*, Kunstchronik, 12th year, 1959, p. 5 ff. — Heinrich WEIZSÄCKER, *Bodensee und Hausbuchmeister*, Jahrbuch für Kunstwissenschaft, 1924-1925, p. 290 ff.

Master of Mondsee: Otto BENESCH, *Der Meister des Krainburger Altars*, Wiener Jahrbuch für Kunstgeschichte, Vol. 8, 1932, p. 36 ff.

Master of the Ortenberg Altarpiece: Gerhard BOTT, *Der Ortenberger Altar in Darmstadt*, Reclam, Stuttgart 1966. (Werkmonographien zur bildenden Kunst. 115.)

Master of the "Paradiesgärtlein": Kurt BAUCH, *Holzschnitte vom Meister des Frankfurter Paradiesgärtleins*, Oberrheinische Kunst, 5th year, 1932, p. 161 ff. — Lilli FISCHEL, *Oberrheinische Malerei im Spiegel des frühen Kupferstichs*, Zeitschrift für Kunstwissenschaft, Vol. I, 1947, p. 23 ff. — Idem, *Eine Strassburger Malerwerkstatt um 1400*, Münchner Jahrbuch der bildenden Kunst, new series, Vol. I, 1950, p. 150 ff. — Idem, *Über die künstlerische Herkunft des Frankfurter "Paradiesgärtleins"*, in *Beiträge für Georg Swarzenski*, Berlin 1951, p. 85 ff. — Ilse FUTTERER, *Eine Gruppe oberrheinischer Tafelbilder des 15. Jahrhunderts*, Oberrheinische Kunst, 2nd year, 1926-1927, p. 15 ff. — Idem, *Zur Malerei des frühen XV. Jahrhunderts im Elsass*, Jahrbuch der preussischen Kunstsammlungen, Vol. 49, 1928, p. 187 ff. — Gustav F. HARTLAUB, *Das Paradiesgärtlein von einem oberrheinischen Meister um 1410*, Berlin 1947. (Der Kunstbrief. 18.) — Walter HUGELSHOFER, *Eine Verkündigung vom Meister des Frankfurter Paradiesgärtleins*, Pantheon, Vol. I, 1928,

p. 66. — Gustav MÜNZEL, *Das Frankfurter Para-diesgärtlein*, Das Münster, 9th year, 1956, p. 14 ff. — Elisabeth WOLFFHARDT, *Beiträge zur Pflanzen-symbolik über Pflanzen des Frankfurter "Paradies-gärtleins"*, Zeitschrift für Kunstwissenschaft, Vol. 8, 1954, p. 177 ff.

Master of Wittingau (or Master of Trebon): Josef CIBULKA, *Rekonstrukce Oltare Trebonského mistra na Zàklade ikonografickém (Rekonstruktion des Altares des Meisters von Trebon [Wittingau] auf ikonographischer Grundlage)*, Umeni, 15th year, 1967, p. 477 ff. (summary in German, pp. 489-491). — Alois ELSEN, *Der Wittingauer Meister und Karl IV.*, Pantheon, Vol. XXIX, 1942, p. 1 ff. — Friedrich Adolf MARTENS, *Wann ist der Wittin-gauer Altar entstanden?*, Zeitschrift des deutschen Vereins für Kunstwissenschaft, Vol. I, 1934-1935, p. 176 ff. — Antonin MATEJCEK, *Mistr Trebonsky (Meister von Wittingau)*, Prague 1937. — Karl OETTINGER, *Der Meister von Wittingau und die böhmische Malerei des späten 14. Jahrhunderts*, Zeitschrift des deutschen Vereins für Kunst-wissenschaft, Vol. I, 1934-1935, p. 293 ff. — Wolfgang STECHOW, *Zur Datierung des "Dritten böhmischen Stils"*, Repertorium für Kunstwissen-schaft, Vol. 52, 1931, p. 70 ff.

Master of 1445: Ernst BUCHNER, *Zwei unbekannte Werke des Meisters von 1445*, Anzeiger für Schwei-zerische Altertumskunde, Vol. 25, 1923, p. 135 ff. — Lilli FISCHEL, *Werk und Name des "Meisters von 1445"*, Zeitschrift für Kunstgeschichte, Vol. 13, 1950, p. 105 ff. — Otto FISCHER, *Der Meister von 1445*, Pantheon, Vol. XIII, 1934, p. 40 ff. — Christian Altgraf SALM, *Die Wandgemälde der Augustinerkirche in Konstanz*, Festschrift Werner Noack, Konstanz and Freiburg im Breisgau, 1959, p. 46 ff. — Idem, *Zur Frage des "Basler Meisters von 1445"*, Kunstchronik, 13th year, 1960, p. 291 ff.

Moser, Lukas: Kurt BAUCH, *Der Magdalenenaltar des Lukas Moser zu Tiefenbronn*, Bremen and Berlin 1940. — Wilhelm BOECK, *Der Tiefenbronner Altar von Lucas Moser*, Munich 1951. — Jörg GAMER, *Zur Rekonstruktion des Magdalenenaltars von Lucas Moser in Tiefenbronn*, Freiburger Diözesan-Archiv, Vol. 74, 1954, p. 195 ff. — Helmut MAY, *Lucas Moser*, Stuttgart 1961. — Johannes Graf von WALDBURG-WOLFEGG, *Lukas Moser*, Berlin 1939.

Multscher, Hans: Julius BAUM, *Zu Multscher*, Das schwäbische Museum, 1928, p. 139 ff. — Otto FISCHER, *Hans Multscher, II: Die Malerei*, Pan-theon, Vol. XXIV, 1939, p. 351 ff. — Kurt GERSTENBERG, *Hans Multscher*, Leipzig 1928. — Nicoló RASMO, *Der Multscher-Altar in Sterzing*, Bolzano 1963. — Franz J. STADLER, *Hans Mult-scher und seine Werkstatt*, Strasbourg 1907. — Rudolf VERRES, *Wo stand Multschers Altar von 1437 ursprünglich?*, in *Festschrift Adolph Gold-schmidt*, Berlin 1935, p. 57 ff.

Pacher, Michael: Johannes VON ALLESCH, *Michael Pacher*, Leipzig 1931. — Otto DEMUS, *Studien zu Michael Pachers Salzburger Hochaltar*, Wiener Jahrbuch für Kunstgeschichte, Vol. 16, 1954, p. 87 ff. — Dagobert FREY, *Michael Pacher-Studien*, Wiener Jahrbuch für Kunstgeschichte, Vol. 15, 1953, p. 23 ff. — Peter HALM, *Michael Pacher. Der Kirchenväter-Altar*, Reclam, Stuttgart 1957. (Werkmonographien zur bildenden Kunst. 19.) — Eberhard HEMPEL, *Michael Pachers Meisterschaft. Zu des Künstlers 500. Geburtstag*,

Pantheon, Vol. 16, 1935, p. 362 ff. — Idem, *Das Werk Michael Pachers*, Schroll, 4th edition, Vienna 1943. — Theodor HOPPE, *Zur Auffindung eines Tafelbildes Michael Pachers*, Wiener Jahrbuch für Kunstgeschichte, Vol. 16, 1954, p. 82 ff. — Laurin LUCHNER, *Die Komposition des Altares zu St. Wolfgang von Michael Pacher*, Beiträge zur Kunst-geschichte Tirols, Innsbruck 1955, p. 85 ff. — Theodor MÜLLER, *Neue Forschungen zu Michael Pacher*, Zeitschrift für Kunstgeschichte, Vol. I, 1932, p. 56 ff. — Otto PÄCHT, *Die historische Aufgabe Michael Pachers*, Kunstwissenschaftliche Forschungen, Vol. I, 1931, p. 95 ff. — Roberto SALVINI, *Sulla posizione storica di Michael Pacher*, Archivio dell'Alto Adige, Vol. 23, 1937, p. 1 ff. — Idem, *La Pittura dell'Alta Italia e la Formazione Artistica di Michael Pacher*, Studi Germanici, I, 1935, p. 631 ff. — Oskar SCHÜRER, *Michael Pacher*, Leipzig 1940. (Knackfuss Künstler-Monographien. 121.) — Hans SEMPER, *Michael und Friedrich Pacher. Ihr Kreis und ihre Nachfolger*, Esslingen 1911. — Robert STIASSNY, *Michael Pachers St. Wolfganger Altar*, Vienna 1919. — Erich STROH-MER, *Michael Pachers Altar in St. Wolfgang am Abersee*, Vienna 1929. — E. D. THEIL-SALMOI-RAGHI, *Michael Pacher in Neustift*, Milan 1946.

Pleydenwurff, Hans: A. FRIESE, *Hans Pleydenwurff. Bildnis des Grafen Georg von Löwenstein*, Kunst-werke der Welt aus dem öffentlichen bayrischen Kunstbesitz, No. 64. — Siegfried WICHMANN, *"Die Auferstehung Christi" aus dem Hofer Altar von Hans Pleydenwurff*, Die Kunst und das schöne Heim, Vol. 55, 1956-1957, p. 241 ff.

Polack, Jan: Alois ELSEN, *Jan Polack, der Münchner Stadtmaler*, Pantheon, Vol. XIX, 1937, p. 33 ff.

Schongauer, Martin: Ludwig BALDASS, *Martin Schon-gauer und die Überwindung des niederländischen Einflusses durch die deutsche Spätgotik*, Reperto-rium für Kunstwissenschaft, Vol. 48, 1927, p. 206 ff. — Kurt BAUCH, *Neues Schrifttum über Martin Schongauer*, Das Münster, 3rd year, 1950, p. 371 ff. — Julius BAUM, *Martin Schongauer*, Schroll, Vienna 1948. — Idem, *Martin Schongauer. Meister und Werkstatt*, in *Meister und Werke spätmittelalterlicher Kunst in Oberdeutschland und der Schweiz*, Lindau and Konstanz, 1957, p. 56 ff. — Ernst BUCHNER, *Martin Schongauer als Maler*, Berlin 1941. — Daniel BURCKHARDT, *Die Schule Martin Schongauers am Oberrhein*, Basel 1888. — Max DVORAK, *Schongauer und die niederländische Malerei*, in *Kunstgeschichte als Geistesgeschichte*, Munich 1923. — Eduard FLECHSIG, *Martin Schon-gauer*, Heitz, Strasbourg 1951. — Max J. FRIED-LÄNDER, *Martin Schongauer*, Berlin 1923. — Kurt MARTIN, *Zur "Madonna im Rosenhang" im Isa-bella-Stewart-Gardner-Museum in Boston*, in *Fest-schrift Werner Noack*, Konstanz and Freiburg im Breisgau, 1959, p. 83 ff. — Idem, *Die Jahreszahl 1473 auf der Rückseite der Maria im Rosenhag von Martin Schongauer*, Annuaire de la Société Historique et Littéraire de Colmar, 11, 1961, p. 25 ff. — Ludwig MOSER, *Der niederländische Lehrer Martin Schongauers*, Das Münster, 4th year, 1951, p. 270 ff. — Herwarth RÖTTGEN, *Zur Stel-lung der Bergheimer Predella in der Kunst des Oberrheins*, Zeitschrift für Kunstwissenschaft, Vol. XIV, 1960, p. 99 ff.

Soest, Conrad von: Exhibition catalogue: *Konrad von Soest und sein Kreis*, Schloss Kappenberg, near Dortmund 1950. — Rolf FRITZ, *Zur westfälischen*

Tafelmalerei um 1400, Zeitschrift Westfalen, Vol. 27, 1948, p. 106 ff. — Idem, *Conrad von Soest. Der Dortmunder Marienaltar*, Bremen 1950. — Idem, *Beobachtungen am Dortmunder Marienaltar Conrads von Soest*, Zeitschrift Westfalen, Vol. 28, 1950, p. 107 ff. — Idem, *Conrad von Soest als Zeichner*, Zeitschrift Westfalen, Vol. 31, 1953, p. 10 ff. — Idem, *Conrad von Soest. Der Wildunger Altar*, Munich 1954. — Max GEISBERG, *Meister Konrad von Soest*, Westfälische Kunsthefte II, Dortmund 1934. — Helmut MAY, *Konrad von Soest. Der Dortmunder Marienaltar*, Diez an der Lahn 1948. — Robert NISSEN, *Die Wiederherstellung der Nikolaustafel in Soest*, Zeitschrift Westfalen, Vol. 18, 1933, p. 228 ff. — Idem, *Ein Beitrag zu Konrad von Soest*, Zeitschrift Westfalen, Vol. 18, 1933, p. 107 ff. — Paul PIEPER, *Zu einer Tafel mit den Heiligen Ottilie und Dorothea*, Zeitschrift Westfalen, Vol. 28, 1950, p. 123 ff. — Theodor RENSING, *Rätsel um Konrad von Soest*, Zeitschrift Westfalen, Vol. 28, 1950, p. 148 ff. — Alfred STANGE, *Eine Tafel von Konrad von Soest*, Wallraf-Richartz-Jahrbuch, new series, Vol. II/III, 1933-1934, p. 165 ff. — Idem, *Konrad von Soest als europäischer Künstler*, Zeitschrift Westfalen, Vol. 28, 1950, p. 101 ff. — Kurt STEINBART, *Konrad von Soest*, Beiträge zur Geschichte Dortmunds und der Grafschaft Mark, Vol. 47, 1948.

Tübingen, Hans von: Karl OETTINGER, *Hans von Tübingen zu Wiener-Neustadt, der Meister von St. Lambrecht*, Jahrbuch der kunsthistorischen Sammlungen in Wien, new series, Vol. VIII, 1934, p. 29 ff. — Idem, *Hans von Tübingen und seine Schule*, Berlin 1938. — Idem, *Hans von Tübingen*, Pantheon, Vol. XXVI, 1940, p. 201 ff.

Wolgemut, Michael: Gerhard BETZ, *Der Nürnberger Maler Michael Wolgemut und seine Werkstatt. Ein Beitrag zur Geschichte der spätgotischen Malerei in Franken*, thesis presented at Freiburg im Breisgau, 1955 (unpublished). — Carl KOCH, *Michael Wolgemut*, Zeitschrift für bildende Kunst, Vol. 63, 1929, p. 81 ff. — Eberhard LUTZE, *Michael Wolgemut (1439-1519)*, Pantheon, Vol. XIII, 1934, p. 262 ff. — Joseph STABER, *Michael Wolgemut in München*, Zeitschrift des deutschen Vereins für Kunstwissenschaft, Vol. VIII, 1941, p. 195 ff. — Wilhelm WENKE, *Das Bildnis bei Michael Wolgemut*, Anzeiger des Germanischen Nationalmuseums, 1932-1933, p. 61 ff. — Carl WILLNAU, *Rogier van der Weyden und Michael Wolgemut*, Die Weltkunst, 24th year, 1954, No. 17 (September 1), p. 7 ff.

Witz, Konrad: Hans AULMANN, *Gemäldeuntersuchungen mit Röntgen-, Ultraviolett- und Infrarotstrahlen zum Werk des Konrad Witz*, Basel 1958. — Julius BAUM, *Der Schrein des Basler Heilspiegel-Altars des Konrad Witz*, in *Meister und Werke spätmittelalterlicher Kunst in Oberdeutschland und der Schweiz*, Lindau and Konstanz 1957, p. 21 ff. — Helmuth T. BOSSERT, *Eine gereimte Erzählung auf den Maler Konrad Witz*, Repertorium für Kunstwissenschaft, Vol. 32, 1909, p. 497 ff. — Adrien BOVY, *Retable de Saint-Pierre*, Compte rendu de l'Administration de la Ville de Genève pour l'Année 1917. — Daniel BURCKHARDT, *Basels Bedeutung für Wissenschaft und Kunst im XV. Jahrhundert*, in *Festschrift zum 400. Jahrestag des ewigen Bundes zwischen Basel und den Eidgenossen*, Basel 1901. — Idem, *Studien zur Geschichte der altoberrheinischen Malerei*, Jahrbuch der königl, preussischen Kunstsammlungen, Vol. XXVII. 1906, p. 1 ff. — Idem, *Aus der Vorgeschichte des Konrad Witz und von den Höhepunkten seiner ersten Basler Tätigkeit*, Zeitschrift für Schweizerische Archäologie und Kunstgeschichte, Vol. 5, 1943, p. 65 ff. — Mela ESCHERICH, *Der Heilsspiegelaltar des Konrad Witz*, Jahrbuch der königl. preussischen Kunstsammlungen, Vol. XXXV, 1914, p. 245 ff. — Idem, *Konrad Witz*, Heitz, Strasbourg 1916. — Otto FISCHER, *Konrad Witz*, Bremen 1938. — Idem, *Konrad Witz*, Schwäbische Lebensbilder, Vol. I, Stuttgart 1940, p. 557 ff. — Idem, *Die künstlerische Herkunft des Konrad Witz*, Pantheon, Vol XXIX, 1942, p. 99 ff. — Joseph GANTNER, *Konrad Witz*, Schroll, Vienna 1942. — Paul Leonhard GANZ, *Meister Konrad Witz von Rottweil*, Berne and Olten 1957. — Hans GRABER, *Konrad Witz*, Basel 1924. — Gustav F. HARTLAUB, *Zwei Detailstudien zur Ikonographie des Magismus in der deutschen Kunst des Spätmittelalters, I: Saturn bei Konrad Witz*, Zeitschrift für Kunstwissenschaft, Bd. X, 1956, p. 23 ff. — Josef HECHT, *Der Aufenthalt des Konrad Witz in Konstanz. Forschungen zur schwäbischen Kunst- und Baugeschichte*, Konstanz 1940. — Hans JANTZEN, *Konrad Witz*, Velhagen und Klasings Monatshafte, 41st year, 1927, p. 139 ff. — Walter JOSEPHI, *Die Verkündigung Mariae im Germanischen Nationalmuseum, ein Werk des Konrad Witz*, Mitteilungen aus dem Germanischen Nationalmuseum, 1910, p. 4 ff. — Emil MAURER, *Konrad Witz und die niederländische Malerei*, Zeitschrift für Schweizerische Archäologie und Kunstgeschichte, Vol. 18, 1958, p. 158 ff. — Idem, *Konrad Witz*, in *Encyclopedia of World Art*, Vol. XIV, New York, 1966, col. 871 ff. — François MAURER, *Die Kunstdenkmäler des Kantons Basel-Stadt*, Vol. IV, Basel 1961, p. 223 ff. — Mathilde MENG-KÖHLER, *Die Bilder des Konrad Witz und ihre Quellen*, Basel 1947. — Herwarth ROTTGEN, *Zwei noch umstrittene Zuschreibungen an Konrad Witz*, Jahrbuch der Berliner Museen, new series, 3, 1961, p. 76 ff. — Fritz SCHMALENBACH, *Kunsthistorische Studien*, privately printed, Basel 1941. — Georg SCHMIDT, *Conrad Witz*, Les Trésors de la Peinture Suisse, Album III, Skira, Geneva 1947. — Idem, *Konrad Witz*, Langewiesche, Königstein/Taunus 1962. — Walter UEBERWASSER *Konrad Witz*, Basel 1938. (Basler Kunstbücher. I.) — Idem, *Konrad Witz und sein Majestas-Altar in Basel*, Kunstchronik, 13th year, 1960, p. 293 ff. — Hans WENDLAND, *Konrad Witz*, Basel 1924.

Zeitblom, Bartholomäus: Carl KOCH, *Zeitbloms reifer Stil*, thesis presented at Berlin, 1909.

General Index

List of Illustrations

THIS VOLUME OF THE COLLECTION "PAINTING - COLOR - HISTORY" WAS
PRODUCED BY THE TECHNICAL STAFF OF EDITIONS D'ART ALBERT SKIRA.
FINISHED THE THIRTIETH OF AUGUST NINETEEN HUNDRED AND SIXTY-EIGHT.

TEXT AND ILLUSTRATIONS PRINTED BY

SKIRA

COLOR STUDIOS

IMPRIMERIES RÉUNIES S.A., LAUSANNE

PLATES ENGRAVED BY GUEZELLE & RENOUARD, PARIS

PHOTOGRAPHS BY

Verlag Karl Alber, Freiburg im Breisgau (page 121), Maurice Babey, Basel (pages 37, 43, 47, 48, 50, 51, 54, 59, 60, 62, 63, 67, 72, 74, 75, 84, 92, 93, 96-97, 99, 105, 108, 109, 110 right, 111, 116, 118, 119, 124, 126, 127, 132, 142, 143, 145), Joachim Blauel, Munich (page 65), Conzett & Huber, Zurich (page 66), U. Edelmann, Frankfurt (page 151 bottom), Farb-Foto-Frank, Salzburg (page 139, 141), John R. Freeman & Co. Ltd, London (page 44), Ernst Matthäus Fürböck, Graz (page 46), Kurt Haase, Bergen-Enkheim (page 98), André Held, Ecublens, Switzerland (pages 22, 25, 30, 34, 36), Hans Hinz, Basel (pages 27, 82, 83, 85, 87, 110 left), Ralph Kleinhempel, Hamburg (pages 31, 58, 107), Timo Liukka, Tapiola (page 56), Erwin Meyer, Vienna (pages 29, 137, 146), Hans Nölter, Hanover (page 32), Herbert Rost, Darmstadt (cover), Schmölz-Huth, Cologne (pages 55, 133, 135), Walter Steinkopf, Berlin (pages 26, 77, 79, 80, 151 top), and the photographic services of the following museums: Colmar, Musée d'Unterlinden (page 150 lower right), Cologne, Wallraf-Richartz Museum (page 136), Darmstadt, Hessisches Landesmuseum (page 150 lower left, 152 top), Gotha, Schlossmuseum (page 122), Helsinki, Suomen Kansallismuseo (page 150 top), Munich, Bayerische Staatsgemäldesammlungen (page 152 bottom, 153 top), Nuremberg, Germanisches Nationalmuseum (page 153 bottom), Stuttgart, Staatsgalerie (page 123).

PRINTED IN SWITZERLAND